THIS IS OUR WORLD

CONQUEST AND CHANGE

First published in this edition 1975
Published by William Collins Sons and Company Limited, Glasgow and London

Printed in Great Britain
ISBN 0 00 106121 6

THIS IS OUR WORLD

CONQUEST AND CHANGE

by Ann Currah
Foreword by James Burke

Collins
Glasgow and London

Contents

Foreword

We live, today, in a world of unparalleled complexity. The flow of information that ought to make that complexity comprehensible has reached the proportions of an uncontrollable torrent. National libraries are unable to say how much is being written, or by whom. The computer has so far been unable to produce a means of providing the general public with access to the information. And yet, access to it becomes more vital, as knowledge becomes more and more specialized.

As the log jam builds up, the development of telecommunications, particularly in the form of television, presents the young people of today with glimpses of a world that their parents already find difficult to cope with. There is increasing concern among the older generation about the need for the kind of information that will enable them to understand and if necessary argue with the changes brought about daily by new developments. It is not that the new knowledge has been deliberately withheld—rather that comprehension demands an ever-increasing expertise in the basic elements of a bewildering number of disciplines.

Again and again in my work I receive letters from parents, and even teachers, asking where they can find the facts that will permit them to explain to their children and pupils why change occurs, and what effects change will have. To such letters, the only possible answer is "read". And yet, where do you go to read, when so many of the thousands of fragmented groups of scientists and thinkers find it so difficult to explain to each other what it is they are doing? There is urgent need, at the adult level, for some kind of common source of data, provided in some common language. Researchers are at present working on such a new language—it's called a meta-language—to answer the problem of translating from English to English.

The dilemma has occurred with the dramatic increase in the sheer number of "things known" over the last half-century. Someone recently said about today's world: "if you understand something it must be obsolete". That is the nub of the problem. The world moves too fast, in too many directions, for anyone to really know more than a tiny fraction of everything there is to know, in any depth. The task, for the adult, is possibly hopeless.

All the more reason that the present-day system of education, which must inevitably equip a child for a career by encouraging specialization, should provide tomorrow's specialist with as wide a grounding in knowledge as possible. It is only with such a broad preparation that tomorrow's specialist will stand a chance of communicating to his fellow members of society. That is why I commend this particular work. It covers an enormously wide variety of subjects, from the nervous system to Alexander the Great and beyond the earth to the stars. Above all, the text is written in such a way as to benefit maximally from use of the way a *child* sees the world. The illustrations are admirably clear, and facts are presented in analogies that a child would use. The work is, I think, a successful attempt to provide easily absorbed, and more important, easily memorable explanations of the world around us. It provides a valuable base on which a young mind can build.

James Burke

Introduction

This book and the companion volumes present a bold, clear picture of the knowledge man has gained about himself, his earth, and the universe he lives in. The text is aimed particularly at young readers of about nine years and upwards.

Here we discuss the rise of mighty empires, great leaders, and powerful ideas which captured the imagination of men. From Alexander the Great, a young man who first ruled the known world, up to the age of the great scientific discoveries and land explorations was a long period of magnificent strides forward in man's history. Learning and scientific discoveries began to change man's way of life; great religious ideas—Christianity and Mohammedanism—influenced the character and actions of thousands. From the early days of Alexander's empire, up through the Middle Ages and the days of castles and knights, was a time when the foundations of the European states were laid.

Young readers' knowledge of these events in man's history is naturally limited. But helping children to draw on and learn new information using their own memories and experience is of great importance in their understanding of man's progress. As we all realize, the simple accumulation of dates, names, places, and events can no longer be a major aim in helping children to learn. What children today need is to be able to adapt to changing states of knowledge, to be able to re-learn and to rethink throughout adult life. This encyclopedia sets out to help children learn to think for themselves. The means employed are simple.

The pictures are large, colourful, specially planned photographs and related drawings. The idea behind them is to draw on children's own knowledge to explain ideas, and to begin to put historical concepts into perspective. For example, the pictures on pages 66 and 67 show the gradual rusting away of tin cans. This is used to explain how the great Roman empire slowly disintegrated. The idea may seem abstruse to adults, but children will catch on quickly to the idea that no profound change occurs overnight.

The man who changed the world

The young prince

For hundreds of years the city-states of Greece had fought fiercely among themselves. At last one man united them under his own rule. He was King Philip of Macedonia, and he had one son, the young prince, Alexander.

A prince must be well-educated, so Philip chose Aristotle, the wisest man in all Greece to teach his son. Aristotle trained Alexander in every branch of human learning. As the young prince grew up, he proved to be both intelligent and brave. There is a famous story about how he tamed his horse, Bucephalus. When Bucephalus was first brought to the royal palace, no one could ride him. Only Alexander realized why. He saw that the horse was frightened by his own shadow. When Alexander mounted Bucephalus, he kept him turned towards the sun until he was calm.

Alexander's bravery was put to the test at an early age. When he was only sixteen years old, his father went away to war, leaving Alexander to guard the kingdom. Before Alexander was twenty, King Philip was murdered. The Greek city-states rose up against Alexander to try to free themselves from Macedonian rule.

The boy king

Alexander wanted to prove that he was as great a king as his father had been. He succeeded because he was a fearless soldier and a brave leader of men. He was also ambitious for power. He brought the Greek city-states under his rule, and then he looked about for other countries to conquer. First, he led a huge war force to Asia Minor. As his fleet drew near the shore of the country we now call Turkey, Alexander stood on the deck of his ship and hurled a spear towards the beach. The spear stuck in the sand. To Alexander, this was a sign that victories in battle would follow.

After conquering Asia Minor, Alexander went on to conquer Phoenicia, on the eastern shores of the Mediterranean sea, Egypt and Mesopotamia (now Iraq). Finally, he defeated the great King Darius of Persia. Then the whole Persian empire belonged to Alexander too.

When he first took over his father's throne, people called Alexander the "boy king." They thought he was too young to hold even the city-states of Greece together. Within a few years, Alexander had proved them wrong. He was no longer the "boy king," he was Alexander the Great.

A soldier and a king

Alexander's success was amazing. He was probably the greatest general history has ever known, for in all his campaigns he never lost a battle. But he was hard on his soldiers. They had to march long, tiring distances in scorching heat. They had to cross mountain ranges in the snow and ice of winter. They had to spend years away from home. On top of all this, they had to fight ferocious battles with powerful enemies. They did not rebel because Alexander himself was such a good soldier. He marched and lived with his men, sharing all their hardships. He did not send his troops into battle and then watch what happened from a safe distance. Instead, he insisted on leading the battles himself. He was often wounded, and once almost died from his injuries. As a result, his men were loyal and would do almost anything for him. Only one campaign was to prove too much for them.

Alexander had always dreamed of conquering India. He led his troops to the Punjab, where they fought the army of a rajah called Porus. This is the first battle we know about in which elephants were used. They were not a great success. They were clumsy, slow to turn, and took up too much room. When frightened they trampled on everyone, friend or foe. In the battle Alexander lost his beloved horse, Bucephalus. Porus was defeated and captured, but his bravery had impressed Alexander. He set the rajah free and gave him back his land.

Then Alexander wanted to go on to the lands across the river Ganges, but his men had had enough. They had beaten Porus with his 200 elephants, but the rulers of the Ganges were said to have 5,000 elephants. Alexander, for once, had to give up and turn back. Of all the troops that had set out with him, only about a quarter of the men returned.

Great generals do not always make wise rulers, but Alexander was both a good soldier and a good king. Although he conquered many lands, he was kind to the people he defeated. He did not make slaves or prisoners of them. On the contrary, he let them worship their own gods, and follow their own ways of life.

Making an empire

Alexander had won himself many lands. Now he had to weld them together – to make them into one empire. It was not an easy job. The peoples of these lands were very different from each other. The peoples of the East knew little about Greece and the West.

One way to join East and West was to encourage people to live and work together. Alexander set a good example by marrying a Persian princess. It is also reported that 10,000 of his soldiers married Persian girls.

Another way to unify people was to spread the Greek language and Greek culture among them. Even during his campaigns, Alexander did this. Greek poets, musicians, artists, and athletes travelled with the troops. Every now and then, Alexander would stop his march and provide entertainments for the wondering eastern peoples.

A third way to unify the empire was to build Greek cities throughout the conquered lands. The greatest of these cities was Alexandria in Egypt.

Alexander also helped to unite his peoples by giving them a god (himself), as well as a king, to obey. In Egypt he travelled into the desert and was accepted by priests as a son of the Egyptian sun god.

In only thirteen years, Alexander spread his rule across the known world and changed it completely. Then, suddenly, he died of a fever.

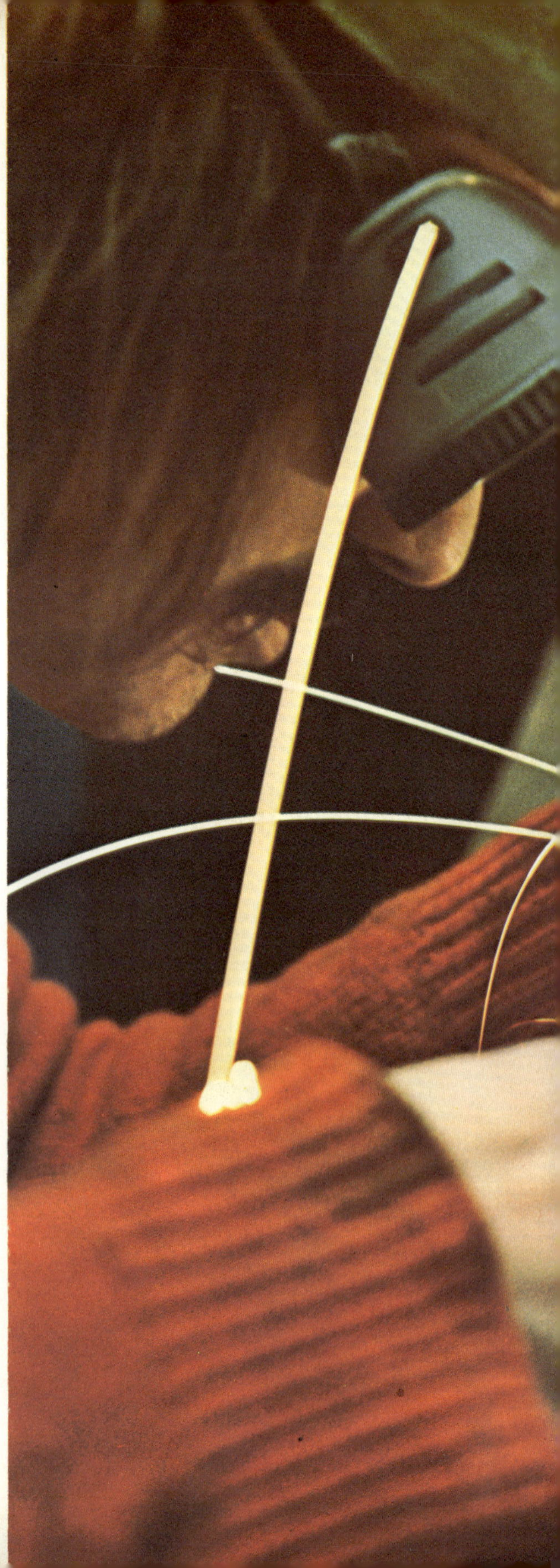

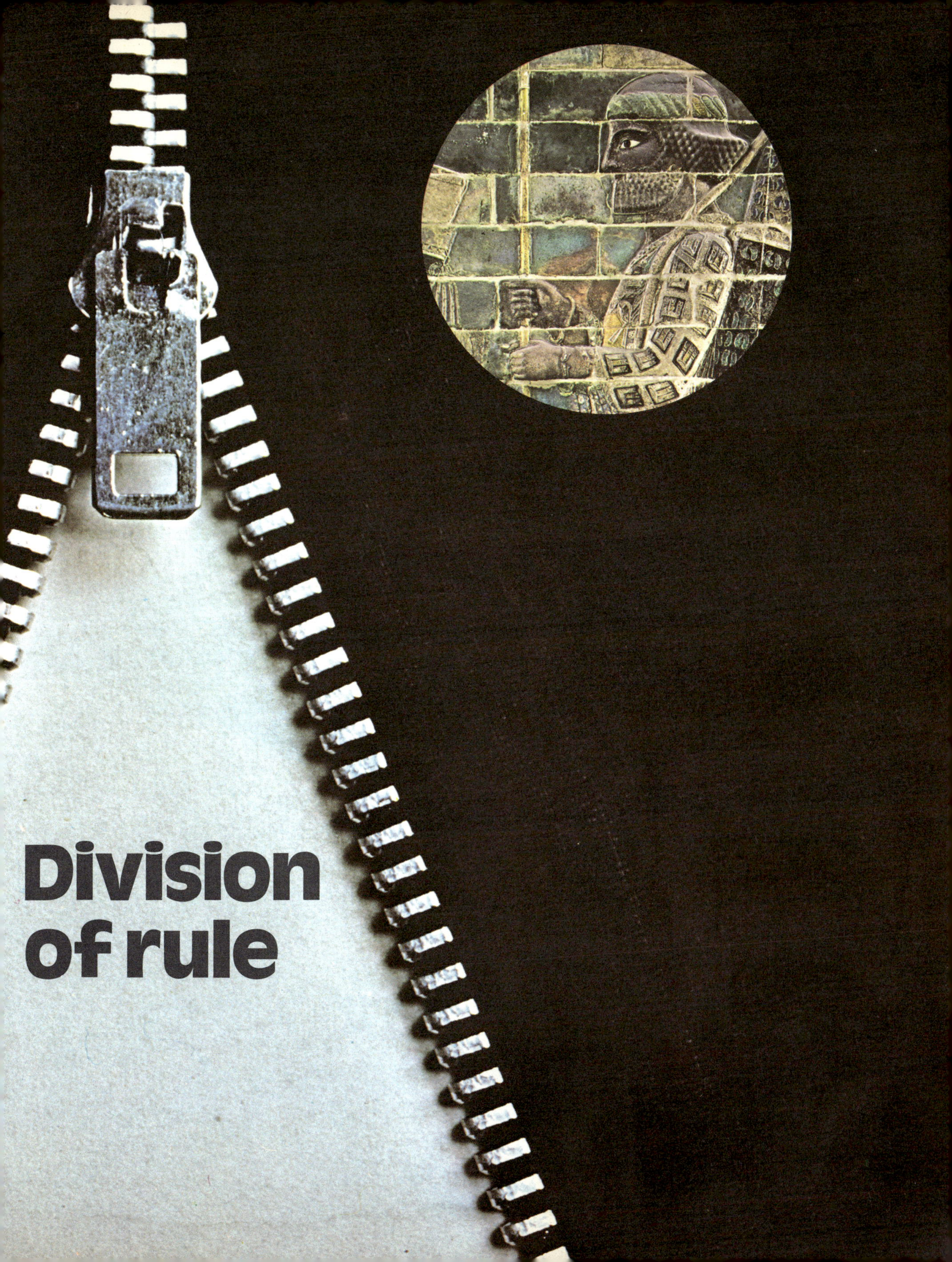

Division of rule

Too many drivers

After Alexander's death no one knew who would take his place. His empire was split up and thrown into total confusion. All his generals found themselves rulers of territories. They began to fight among themselves, each one hoping to win the whole empire for himself. Ambitious soldiers grabbed important jobs, but quickly lost them again. Some sold cities and even whole provinces to their men when they had no money to pay their wages. At sea and on land army fought army, across Europe, Africa, and Asia. Macedonia was overrun by tribes, called Celts, from Central Europe. In Greece, the city-states tried to band together. They formed two leagues, but even the leagues could not agree with each other.

Alexander's great empire had become like a vehicle with too many people trying to drive it. As each one tried to steer it this way and that, the whole thing fell to pieces.

This struggle went on for forty years. Many of the generals were defeated or killed. At last, the empire was divided among those who were left. Three new kingdoms slowly came into being. These were Macedonia, ruled by Antipater; Asia, ruled by Seleucus; and Egypt, ruled by Ptolemy. East was split from West once more, and yet there was still a link between them. That link was Greek civilization.

A taste of the world

For hundreds of years the Greeks kept themselves to themselves. They were too busy fighting each other to venture into the outside world. Before the birth of Alexander they had only nibbled at the known. Under Alexander, they managed to swallow up almost all of it. Greek learning, art, and ideas spread from the Danube river in the northwest to the river Indus in the southeast. This was the known world, for Alexander did not know there was such a place as China. The Greek word for their own country is Hellas, and they call themselves Hellenes. The world Alexander left behind is known as Hellenistic.

One thing the Greeks taught other people was how to govern. The word for Greek city-state is *polis*. From this comes our own word politics, meaning the science of government. The Greeks invented this science. In Athens, every male citizen had a vote. In other words, there was government by the people, or democracy.

Greek writers helped to spread Greek ideas. Few books were written for reading to oneself. The Greeks wrote poems to be read aloud or to be set to music. As their language spread, many more people could enjoy these. They could also watch the wonderful comic or tragic Greek plays. The tragic plays (tragedies) made people feel pity or terror. The comic plays (comedies) were a mixture of wit, poetry, and song.

The Greeks also spread their ideas about education and learning. Just as children do today, Greek children went to school. They sat on stools, resting writing tablets on their knees. They learned reading, writing, mathematics, and painting. Sports were important, and so was music. Children learned to play a lyre, which was an instrument like a harp.

Wise and learned Greek men did not specialize in any one kind of learning. For example, Alexander's teacher, Aristotle, studied science, law, and politics. Learned men like Aristotle were called philosophers, which means they studied wisdom. Wisdom means being wise, and wisdom was the Greeks' greatest gift to the Hellenistic world.

A light for the world

The city of learning

After Alexander's death, Egypt was the most firmly ruled of the three new kingdoms. King Ptolemy had been one of Alexander's greatest generals. Like Alexander, he had been taught by Aristotle. He wanted Alexandria to lead the world in science and learning. Unfortunately, Ptolemy was seldom left in peace. Much of his reign was spent in defending his kingdom. In spite of this, he and the Ptolemies who came after him made Alexandria a great city. Not only the centre of world trading, Alexandria was also the centre of Greek culture. The splendid intellectual life of this great city centred round its museum.

Chief port for Egypt it was to Alexandria that everyone came. Doctors, mathematicians, astronomers, engineers, and architects were all encouraged to live and work in Alexandria. So too were poets, painters, sculptors, and craftsmen.

The light of learning burned brightly in Alexandria, and so did another great light. This was the Pharos, the first lighthouse in the world. Standing 134 metres (440 feet) high, it was one of the seven wonders of the ancient world. The glow of its flames could be seen from more than 48 kilometres (30 miles) away. It was destroyed by an earthquake in the fourteenth century.

The world's library

All the learned men working and studying in Alexandria needed books. They also needed somewhere to read, to write, and to carry out all kinds of research or study. To meet this need, Ptolemy I built a great museum and library. The museum was not like the kind we have today. Nowadays, we would call it a Research Institute. In its wonderful library, the Ptolemies tried to collect all the books in the known world.

In the ancient world, books were not made of flat sheets of paper bound together. Each book was a large sheet of papyrus, a kind of paper made by Egyptians from the stems of water reeds. Some books were 45 metres (150 feet) long. All the sheets of papyrus were kept neatly rolled up.

Scribes or writers from all over the world sailed to Alexandria to work in the library. There was no way then of printing books in great numbers, as there is today. Instead, each copy of a book had to be carefully written out by hand.

Food for thought

The word museum means a place sacred to the Muses, nine Greek goddesses of the arts and sciences. The museum at Alexandria had a temple to the Muses. There were also anatomy theatres where doctors could study the human body. There were gardens and a zoo for the study of plants and animals. For those who were interested in the planets, there was an observatory from which to view the skies. All the museum's scholars were paid by the kings.

The scholars had a dining hall, where they met to eat. The food set before them would probably seem strange to us now. Wheat and barley were staple foods. These would either be boiled up as porridge or baked into bread. The bread was used to scoop up other food. The scholars may have eaten soup made with beans, peas, or lentils, followed perhaps by a kind of black pudding. To drink they would have sheep or goat's milk, or wine. Beef was scarce and expensive, but fish was often eaten. Meals would finish with fruit or cakes sweetened with honey.

To the Greeks, talking was always more important than eating. Perhaps, in the museum, the words tasted better than the food.

The first doctors

The Greeks were the first people to think of medicine as a science. The first great doctor was Hippocrates, who is said to have lived for over a hundred years. Doctors today still follow some of his rules.

The Greeks brought their medical science to Alexandria, where the first great medical school was built. It was a good place to set up a school of medicine because the Egyptians did not feel that it was wrong to cut up (or dissect) human bodies. It was their practice to embalm the dead and to do this they had to open up the bodies to put in preserving spices. So, doctors at Alexandria were able to dissect and find out many important things about the human body.

One of the beliefs of the doctors who followed Hippocrates was that the body had "humours" or special substances. They said the body had four humours: blood (red), phlegm (white), choler (yellow), and melancholy (black bile). When someone was ill, they said he had too much of one humour. Look at the figures shown here. Each of the first four shows too much of one humour. The fifth figure shows perfect health. We no longer believe in humours, but we still refer to them. We say that someone is phlegmatic, meaning he is cool and calm. Or we say that someone else is melancholy, meaning that he is sad and unhappy.

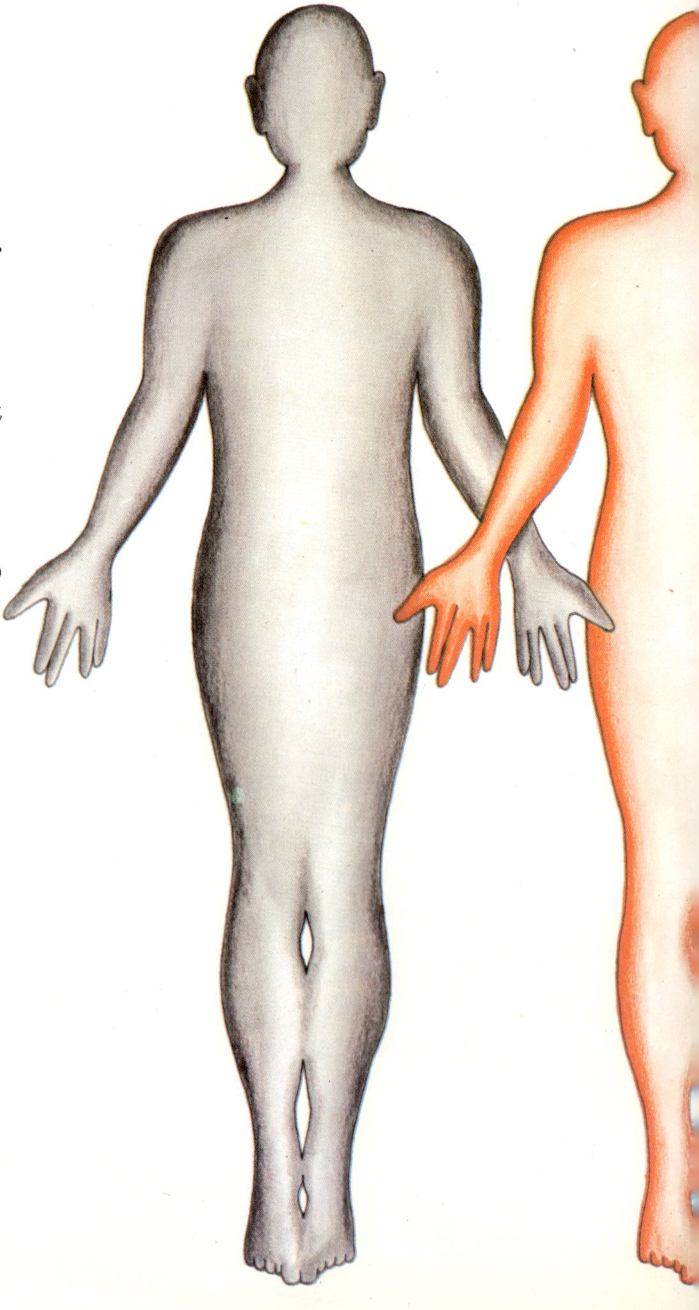

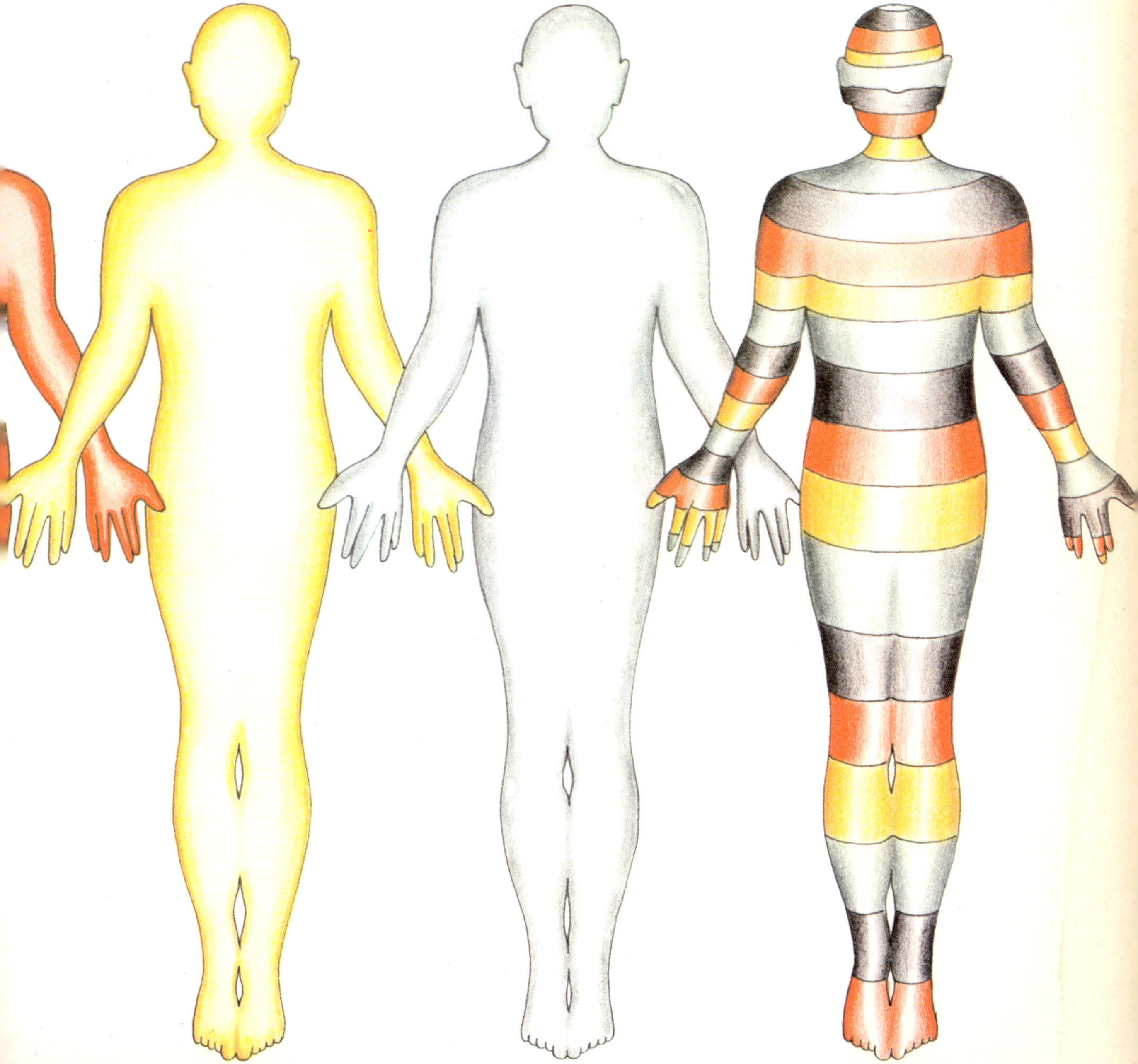

Measuring the earth

Eratosthenes, the librarian at Alexandria, was the first man to measure the earth. He saw that the midday sun reflected in a well at Syrene (now Aswan in Egypt) was directly overhead. But at Alexandria, 800 kilometres (500 miles) away, he saw that an upright rod cast a small shadow at midday. Eratosthenes measured the angle at which the sun's rays fell on the rod. A full circle measures 360°. The angle Eratosthenes measured was one-fiftieth of that. Therefore, he thought, the distance from Syrene to Alexandria must be one-fiftieth of the earth's measurement. Fifty times 800 is 40,000 kilometres (25,000 miles). Although his method was simple, Eratosthenes was correct to within 160 kilometres (100 miles).

Seas and tides

The men who marched with Alexander the Great not only conquered they also explored and discovered. Scientists as well as soldiers travelled with him. And so the library at Alexandria had some of the first accurate information about the earth's geography.

Coming from the shores of the Mediterranean, the scientists were used to a gentle rise and fall in the level of the sea. Imagine their surprise at the sight of the great tidal movements of the oceans. The Mediterranean Sea is almost surrounded by land and so has little tidal rise and fall. Today we know that the oceans' rise and fall (tides) is caused by the sun and the moon. The pull of gravity, mainly from the moon, and the rotation, or turning, of the earth makes tides happen.

Tides act strangely in some parts of the world. On the English and Dutch coasts, on opposite sides of the North Sea, it is high tide on the one while there is low tide on the other. Some places have more tides than others; these are good places for big ports. Southampton and Le Havre each have six tides a day. Tides can produce odd effects, as at Mont St Michel in France. This hill is joined to the mainland at low tide, but at high tide it is almost an island.

The earth that breathed

When Eratosthenes was alive, people did not know about the pull of gravity. They thought the earth behaved like a living being. When earth breathed in, the seas rose. When it breathed out again, the seas fell. Because we know better, this seems funny to us. But the scholars at Alexandria were anxious to know more about the earth. They wanted to make an accurate map of it. The library was given money specially for this purpose, and it was Eratosthenes who had to carry out the task. To do it he used his knowledge of mathematics, geography, and astronomy. He also had the reports of travellers, merchants, and soldiers to help him.

The remarkable thing about Eratosthenes' map was that he divided it up with a grid of horizontal and vertical lines. If you

look at a modern map, you will see that grid lines are still used. The little squares on the map are the grid. The centre of Eratosthenes' map was Alexandria. He drew his main horizontal line through it, calling it the Parallel of Alexandria. Then he drew a vertical line through it, and called that the Meridian of Alexandria. The map went about as far north as the British Isles, and about as far south as the Arabian Gulf. From Ireland in the west, it went east to the Ganges, and included the island we now call Ceylon (Sri Lanka). To Eratosthenes, this was the habitable world, the only area in which people could live. Less than a hundred years later, a map was drawn that went as far south as the Mountains of the Moon in Africa, as far north as Russia, and as far east as China.

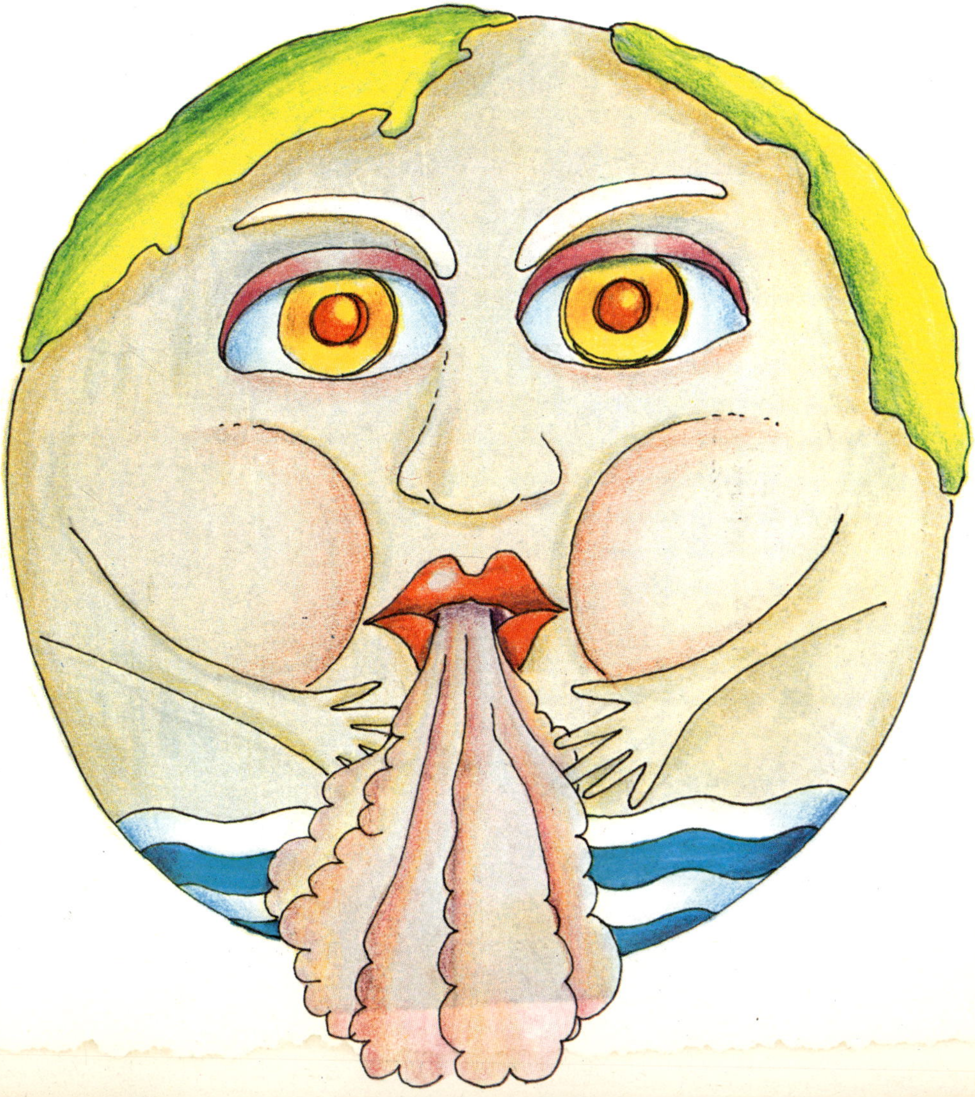

Inventions and discoveries

The famous school of mathematics at Alexandria was probably started by a man named Euclid. We know only a little about Euclid's life, but his work was very important. He studied geometry, the science of lines and surfaces and solids. His writings about geometry are still used in schools today. Another great mathematician was Archimedes, who was born in Syracuse in Sicily. He visited Egypt and knew Eratosthenes. Archimedes invented a screw or a type of primitive pump for lifting water from one level to another. The Nile river farmers still use this type of screw today. Archimedes also invented war machines.

Hero of Alexandria was a mathematician who invented many machines. He built a globe that whirled round by force of steam. This idea led many years later to the steam engine. Hero also invented a pump for a fire engine.

Many inventions in the Hellenistic age were clever but not very useful. Hero invented a way to open temple doors using heated air. Another invention was a water organ, a mass of water forced air through tubes which created musical sounds. Useful inventions were the lever, the mill, the windlass, and the pump, and even a speedometer.

Rome – a city, a republic

A bridge to Rome

For a long time the Greeks were the most important people in the ancient world. But other peoples became powerful too. Among them were the Etruscans, who lived in north and central Italy. Where they first came from we do not know. Probably they travelled by sea from Asia Minor. They traded with the Greeks, and learned from them. The Greeks and Romans did not like the Etruscans. They accused them of being pirates, and perhaps they were.

Etruscan paintings show us a people who lived in gaily decorated houses and who loved feasting and dancing. The figures shown here decorated a stone coffin, or sarcophagus. The couple look very relaxed, and were probably feasting. Like the Greeks and the Romans the Etruscans, when they were eating, reclined like this, supported on the left elbow.

The Etruscans were a war-like people. They defeated Rome when it was still a small settlement, and for a time they ruled it. Then Rome grew stronger and swallowed up Etruscan civilization. But it was not entirely lost. The Etruscans made the great drainage works of Rome, and taught the Romans much about building. The great civilization of Rome was based on a blending of Greek and Etruscan culture.

The birth of the republic

There is a legend about the founding of Rome. It is said that twin babies, Romulus and Remus, were thrown into the river Tiber by their wicked great uncle. The babies were rescued by a she-wolf, who became their foster-mother. They grew up to found the city of Rome, and Romulus was its first king. After Romulus, came seven more kings, and the last three of these were Etruscan. A revolution

overthrew the last king, and Rome then became a republic, governed by the people.

The early Romans were a mere few thousand peasants, farming the seven small hills beside the Tiber. They were constantly attacked, and many of their enemies were rich and powerful. At first, it was a case of peasants fighting well-paid soldiers. But the Roman army of farming people was loyal and well-organized. They gradually defeated all their enemies, and came to control the whole Mediterranean world.

Rich and poor

The Etruscan kings started a system of dividing the people of Rome into two groups, or classes. The first was the patrician class. To this belonged all the rich, powerful people who owned land. The second was the plebian class, to which belonged all the

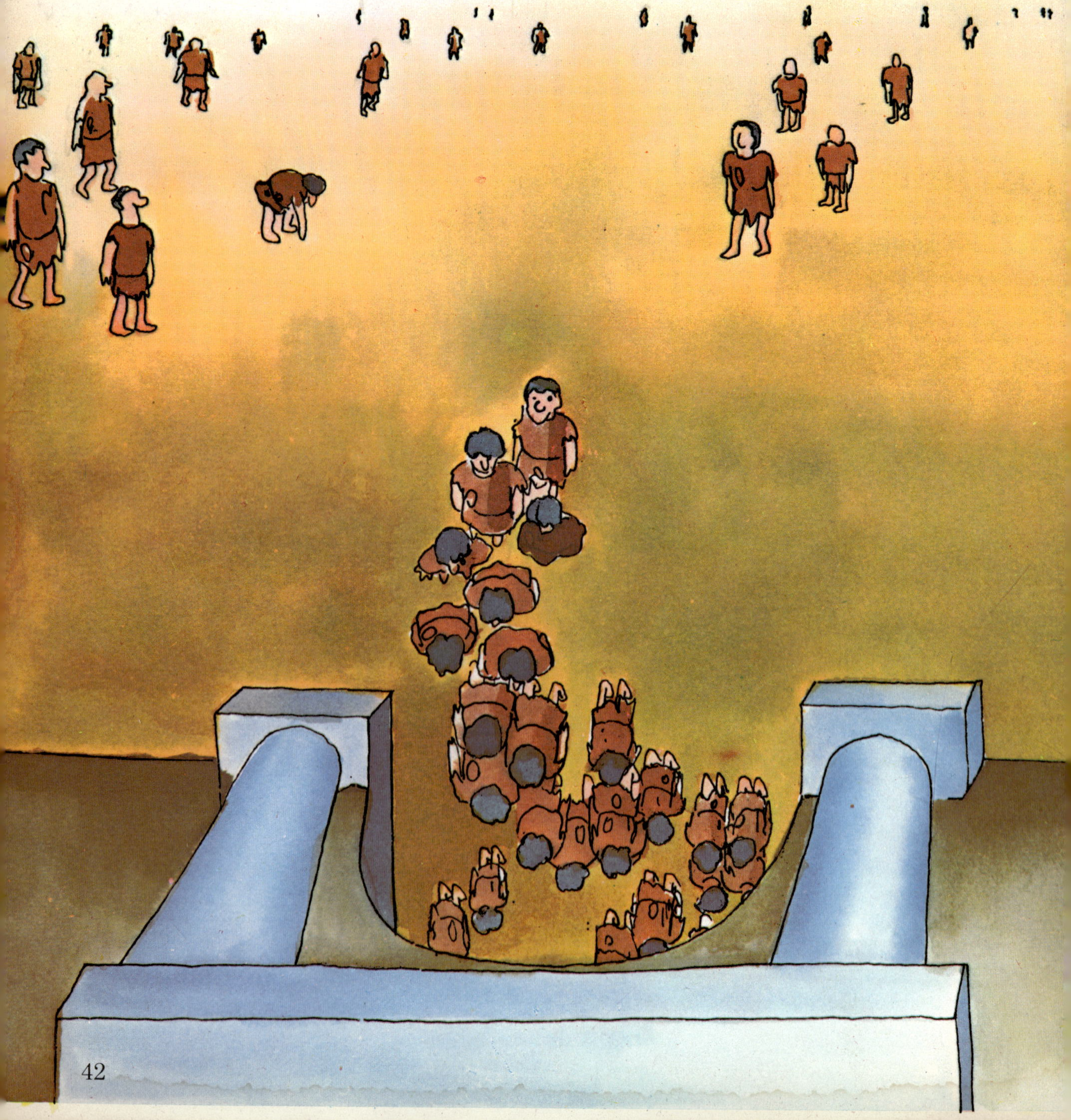

ordinary working people. Plebians could become rich if they were, perhaps, successful traders, but they could not become powerful. There was a third group of people in Rome. They were the slaves, but they were not thought of as people at all. They were useful domestic animals, like the oxen that pulled the carts.

The senate

The patricians were the only people who could hold power in Rome. Probably it was the patricians who overthrew the king and formed a republic. Afterwards, they made up the senate, which governed the people.

Every year, the senate voted for two magistrates, whose job it was to see that the laws of the land were obeyed. These magistrates were known as Consuls. They were the supreme heads of state, both in peace, and in war. The details of daily life were controlled by the Senate. In particular the soldiers, or legionaries, had to do exactly as the Senate pleased.

Senators treated legionaries like puppets, with little concern for their wishes. This was foolish, for Rome depended on the army. The legionaries were unhappy, and in time grew angry at their treatment.

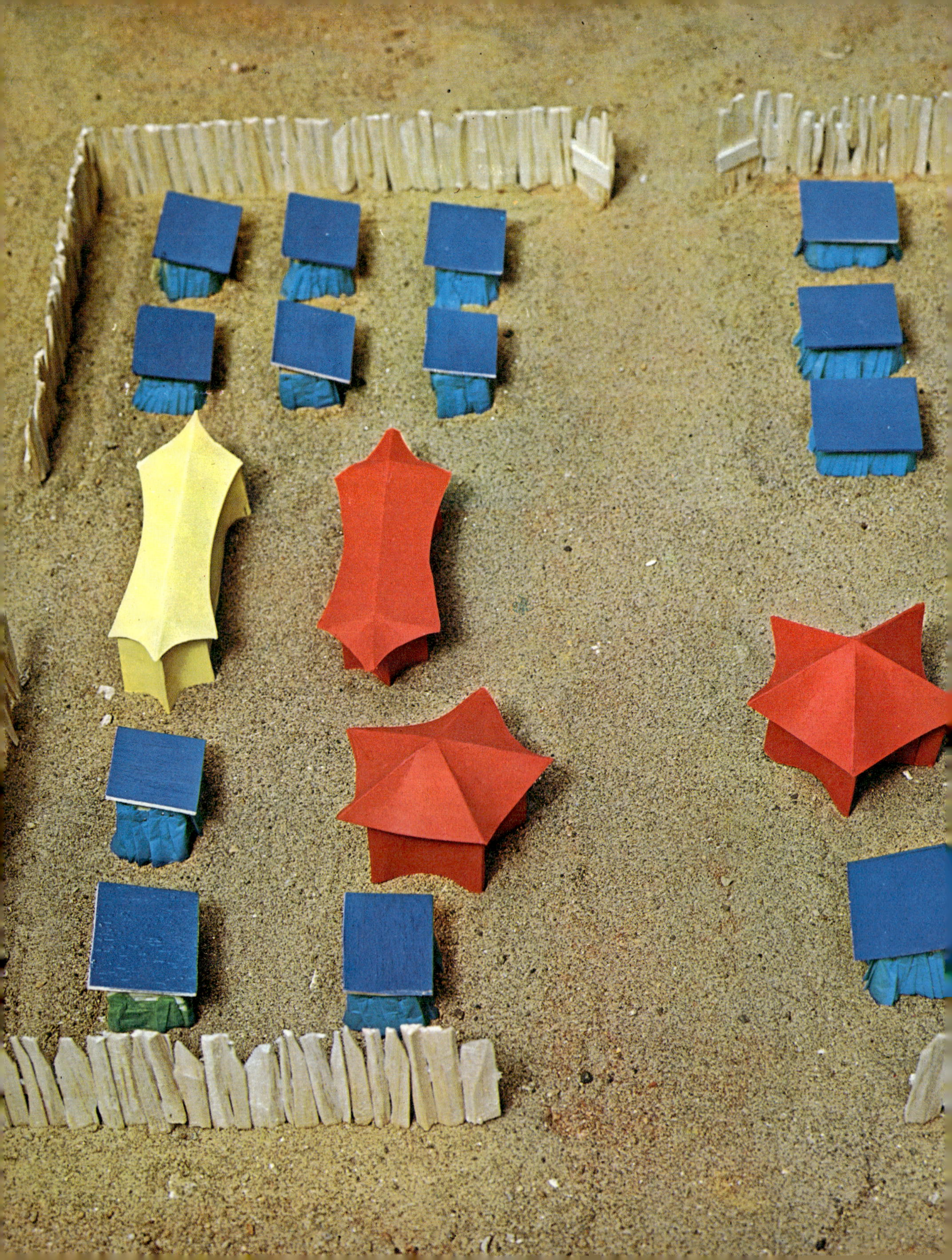

Wars and conquests

After the Romans defeated the Etruscans, they gradually came to control the rest of Italy. They even conquered the Greeks of the south. The Romans did not allow any of the cities they conquered to trade with each other. Instead they had to trade only with Rome. In this way, the Romans kept control of their colonies. More and more people in Italy were proud to call themselves citizens of Rome.

While Rome was taking over Italy, the western part of the Mediterranean was under the rule of Carthage. This Phoenican city in North Africa had built up a great trading empire. The Phoenicians had always been sailors, so in order to defeat them the Romans had to learn to fight at sea. This they did, and after a long struggle defeated the Phoenicians. Then a Carthaginian general, Hannibal, invaded Italy. In an amazing journey, he crossed the Alps, with a vast army and a train of elephants. Again, after many battles, Rome was victorious.

By the end of the republic, Rome had provinces in Spain, southern France, Greece, Sicily, Corsica, Sardinia and present-day Tunisia. Later, the Roman empire included all the lands round the Mediterranean. The Rhine and the Danube were its northern limits, and even Britain was part of the empire, as far north as Hadrian's Wall.

Too many people

As Rome grew richer, more and more people crowded into the city. Like mushrooms springing up overnight, houses appeared everywhere. Overcrowding leads to slums. So what the Romans had to undertake was a slum clearance scheme. They did this, and they also began to build splendid new public buildings. Because of the number of people these buildings had to hold, they had to be bigger than any such buildings had ever been. So architects and builders had to look for new materials and new methods. To put domed roofs across enormous areas, they had to use brick and concrete in huge rounded arches.

An important development was the use of the basilica, a kind of rectangular hall with pillars. In Rome a basilica was built onto the open market place, or forum. It was used as a kind of civic centre. Later, early Christians built basilicas as churches.

In this city of splendid temples, baths, theatres, and triumphal arches, ordinary people had to live in blocks of flats. The price of land was so high that only the rich could afford houses with gardens. The flats were often six storeys high, with balconies, and had no private lavatories. Because of the great risk of fire and collapse, laws were made controlling the height of buildings. Luckily, Rome had both firemen and a police force.

Days of the empire

One man rules

A republic has a government elected by the people. An empire is ruled by one man, usually the emperor.

Why did Rome change from a republic to an empire? As Rome won more colonies, rich citizens grew richer. Small farms went out of existence because it was easier for Rome to bring in grain than to grow it. The land was taken over by the rich for their estates. Out-of-work peasants flocked to Rome. But there was no work for them there because too many slaves had been brought in from North Africa. A civil war started—a kind of war in which the people of a country fight each other. After a struggle lasting about one hundred years, one man became ruler of Rome. He did not call himself the emperor, but that is what he was. His name was Julius Caesar.

Roman roads

As the Roman empire grew larger and larger, people needed to travel easily to all parts of it. Orders and supplies had to be taken to legionaries guarding distant lands. Letters and goods had to be sent back and forth, or there was a danger of far-off provinces becoming cut off from Rome.

To avoid this, good roads had to be built. Roman road builders laid very good foundations. They put down many layers of rocky material. On top of this they put a heavy layer of stones, which they cemented in place. Roads like this were so good that many are still in use today.

The Romans did not like their roads to run up and down hill. They liked them to be as straight as possible. Where there was a hill, they dug a tunnel through it. Where there was a valley they crossed it by putting the road on a bridge, or on a viaduct. Many of these tunnels and viaducts are also still in use. A Roman viaduct can be recognized by its beautiful rounded arches.

Distances on Roman roads were marked every 1,000 double steps (about 1,600 metres or 1,620 yards) by a milestone like the one in the picture. Each milestone bore the name of the emperor then in power.

Words and pictures

Whenever the Romans were particularly fond of something, they wrote poems about it and painted pictures of it. One of the things they loved best was beautiful countryside. The writer Pliny tells us about walls in houses and buildings painted with "gardens, groves, hills, fish ponds." The great poet Virgil wrote about the countryside. Many of his facts came from a book written for farmers, but that did not spoil the beauty of his poems. Virgil's poems have led other poets to write about nature and inspired artists to paint pictures of the scenes he described.

Buried treasure

One terrible summer day in the year AD 79, three Roman towns were completely buried. The towns were Pompeii, Herculaneum, and Stabiae. They were built on the slopes of Mount Vesuvius. People knew that Vesuvius was a volcano, but they thought it was extinct, or dead. Then, suddenly, it erupted, spilling out flames and lava, or molten rock. The writer Pliny was in command of the Roman fleet, which was nearby. Anxious to see what was happening, he sailed towards Vesuvius. As the ships drew near, showers of red-hot stones fell on them. Pliny landed, but thick clouds of smoke drove him back.

The three towns disappeared beneath the volcanic ash. No one saw them again for almost 2,000 years. When they were at last uncovered, they were found to be still quite perfect. People who visit them now can walk along Roman streets, looking at the shops, houses, and cafes. They can go into family homes, and see the furniture, the beautiful wall paintings, the children's toys, and the cooking pots still on the stoves. There is even a baker's shop with the loaves still in the oven.

Everything is still exactly as it was on the 23rd of August, in AD 79. The burial of Pompeii and the other towns was a disaster, but it has allowed us, hundreds of years later, to see exactly how the Romans lived.

Roman towns

We know quite a lot about Roman towns and what it was like to live in them. Many of the things we take for granted today, like heating, lighting, and cleanliness, were luxuries for the Romans. Their streets were filthy and dark. Inside the houses small lamps burned olive oil or candles made of tallow (hard fat). Poor people did not burn many lights, for both oil and tallow were food. We know too that the Romans bought a lot of eye medicine. Perhaps the dust and dirt hurt their eyes, or maybe they overtired them by working in bad light. In a really cold spell, everyone froze except

those who were rich enough to have charcoal-burning stoves. There was no coal, but some important buildings had central heating, with large wood-burning furnaces under the floors.

To bring water into their towns, the Romans built aqueducts, or bridges, which carried water above the ground. Rich people could have it piped right into their houses. Rich and poor alike went to bathe at the public baths. There they could swim in hot or cold pools, meet their friends, walk in the gardens, and buy food and drink. Roman towns even had free medical care—doctors and hospitals looked after poor people and the medical fees were paid by the town.

Sports and games

Like children today, Roman children played leap-frog and hide-and-seek. They also played with balls, hoops and tops and, when adult, watched games and shows of all kinds. Just as people today watch games or sports events, Romans watched gymnastic displays and went to the theatre.

Throughout the Roman empire there were great arenas, but the most splendid sports stadium ever built was the Colosseum in Rome. Its opening day was a public holiday. For weeks before, posters had announced the names of the stars who were to appear. Although at the time many Romans were out of work, hungry, or angry with the government, the emperor had the great arena built to amuse and keep the people quiet. Hunters were sent to Africa to catch wild animals. In the Colosseum, screaming crowds watched the animals fight and kill. Gladiators, or paid fighters, fought to the death with spears and nets, and tridents (three-pronged spears). The arena was even filled with water, so that battles could be fought with ships. To make them even more excited, sometimes the people watching were showered with gold coins. So popular were these shows that the Colosseum was not large enough to hold all the people who wanted to attend. Also in Rome, at the Circus Maximus, 350,000 people could watch chariot-racing.

CASTROL CASTROL CASTROL CASTROL
Shell
ROTHMANS
DAILY EXPRESS
HAIG WHISKY
FERODO
Motor
CASTROL
CASTROL CASTROL CASTROL
ROTHMANS

The emperors

When Roman generals won great victories abroad, they returned loaded with gold and jewels to offer to the emperor. They also brought chained prisoners to be sold as slaves. The great wealth of the Roman emperors was built on these stolen riches, and on the unpaid work of the slaves.

The first emperor was Octavian, great-nephew of Julius Caesar. He was known as the Emperor Augustus. Every time we write down the date we

acknowledge Julius Caesar and Augustus, for they gave us the calendar we still use today. Augustus was a great and wise ruler. It is said that he found Rome built of brick and left it built of marble. Some emperors were hated and feared, like Caligula, whose name means "little boots." Romans went in terror of him until he was murdered after ruling only four years. The most hated emperor of all was Nero. He blamed the Christians for starting the fire in which two-thirds of Rome was burned to the ground.

The first Christians

Early man worshipped the rivers, trees and the sun because he believed they had special powers. Then he carved gods out of stone or wood. Soon some early peoples believed that there was one god above all others—that there was a creator of life on earth.

The early Jews believed in one god, the father of man and life. They also believed they were specially chosen by God and that He gave them a set of laws to guide their conduct as Jews. These laws were the Ten Commandments. The Jews too looked forward to a special person, called the Messiah, who would come from heaven to save them and the world.

When Jesus of Nazareth was born some people thought He was this special person, the Messiah. The Jewish leaders saw him as a threat to their leadership, and so they conspired to get rid of him. Jesus was accused of having called Himself the King of the Jews. The Romans ruled the Holy Land at this time and they too were afraid of a man like Jesus who might lead people to revolt against Rome. So Jesus was put to death upon a cross. Then his followers claimed He came to life again. Paul, who had at first attacked the early Christians, met Jesus in a dream, and decided he must travel round teaching everyone that Jesus was alive. Many people listened to Paul on his travels. Jews, Greeks, and Romans became converted to the new faith and to belief in Jesus the Messiah. They became the first Christians.

Nero was the first emperor to persecute (hunt down or put to death) the Christians. He hated them because they didn't treat him as a god. The Christians had to hide from his hate in the Roman catacombs. These were caves where Romans buried their dead. In the catacombs and elsewhere, the Christians used secret signs to show their faith. The most important sign was the fish. In Greek, the first letters of the words Jesus Christ, son of God, spell a word that means fish. So the fish became a symbol of the Saviour or the Messiah.

The empire dies

Rome rusts away

Over hundreds of years, the power of the great Roman empire slowly lessened. Like a bright, shining piece of metal, it looked good on the outside but there were a few specks of rust. Slowly, as rust spreads, metal grows thinner and crumbles away. The Roman empire crumbled away and one of the causes was its sheer size. The Romans took over so much of the world that it was impossible for them to defend it properly. In an age when there were no cars, trains, or planes it took a long time to travel from one part of the world to another. Even to send a letter asking for help took a long time. Today a tourist might visit France, Italy, Spain, Greece, or North Africa. He might travel as far as Turkey, Iraq, or Arabia. He would find these places strange and exciting, and all the different languages hard to understand. For a Roman, all these places, and more besides, were simply different parts of his own empire. Wherever he went, he would feel quite at home. All the towns looked much alike, with the same kind of baths,

theatres, market places, and temples. Most people he met could speak his own language, Latin, or if not they could speak Greek.

When we think of the size of the Roman empire in this way, it does not seem strange that it crumbled away. It seems much stranger that it held together for so long.

A great empire cannot be governed well from a city that is troubled. In Rome, as the rich grew richer and the poor grew poorer, civil wars broke out. Because their pay was bad the army had too few soldiers, so emperors took land and money away from their rightful owners to pay the army. People grew even angrier. Still there were not enough soldiers, so foreigners, called barbarians, were brought into the army. To make things worse, Rome was struck with the plague, a dreadful disease. Governors of far-off districts rebelled against Rome. Barbarians attacked many parts of the empire, and it was hard to defeat them when the army itself was full of barbarians. Soldiers not only killed the enemy, they killed their own generals too.

One emperor, Diocletian, tried to stop the rust and make Rome strong again. He believed that the new religion was one of the things that had made Rome weaker. Under his rule, Christians suffered even more than before. But once rust has started it is very hard to stop. For the Roman empire, the end was in sight.

Constantine the Great

In spite of Diocletian, governing the huge Roman empire became more and more difficult. Things became really absurd when there were actually six emperors at one and the same time. At last, one strong man—Constantine, the emperor of the Western empire—took control. Although so many of the Christians had been put to death, the faith of those who were left was still strong. Constantine joined them. Along with Licinius, emperor of the East, he issued the Edict of Milan. This was a law in favour of the Christians, giving them freedom to practise their religion. Not long afterwards, Constantine fell out with Licinius and defeated him. Constantine became the only ruler of the Roman world. He moved his capital from Rome to the old city of Byzantium. There he made a splendid new city, called Constantinople (today it is called Istanbul, and it is the capital of Turkey). Constantinople was the first Christian city.

The barbarians

The word "barbarian" was invented by the Greeks, and later used by the Romans. At first it simply meant "foreigner." The Greeks and Romans did not like foreigners. They found them ignorant, for they knew nothing of the arts and sciences. They thought foreign habits primitive and cruel, compared with their own. Gradually, the word barbarian came to mean anyone ignorant, savage, and generally unpleasant. All the tribes of German peoples north of the River Danube, where the Roman empire ended, were known to the Romans as barbarians. We know very little of their early history, but we believe they came from icy regions in the far north of Europe. Some stayed there, and their descendants are the present-day Norwegian, Swedish, and Danish people. Others were nomads, or wanderers. Two of the western tribes, the Saxons and the Franks, finally settled in Britain and France. The eastern tribes were called the Goths and the Vandals. These German peoples had a good reason for forcing their way into the Roman empire. They were themselves fleeing from different barbarians, the Huns. Under their leader Attila, the Huns swept out of central Asia, killing everyone who got in their way. Romans and Germans joined together to fight them. Then, weakened by the struggle, Rome itself fell to the Goths and Vandals.

The rough and the smooth

For a time Constantine and the emperors who came after him, ruled the whole empire from Constantinople. Then, on the death of the emperor Theodosius I, the empire was divided between his two sons. Honorius ruled the West from Italy, and Arcadius ruled the East from Constantinople. The East had always been stronger and richer than the West. After the division, the eastern, or Byzantine empire, turned its back on the troubles of the West. Honorius was a weak emperor. He could not defend Rome against the attacks of Alaric the Goth. After Honorius, eleven more weak emperors ruled in the West. Barbarians took away more and more of the empire until there was almost nothing left except part of Italy. Rome began with Romulus and it almost finished with Romulus. The last emperor, Romulus Augustulus was a fourteen-year-old boy.

When he was overthrown, the great Roman empire was truly at an end.

Although we call all the peoples who took over the western Roman empire barbarians, this does not mean that they were all the same. They were not all ignorant savages, nor were they all trying to destroy Roman civilization. They were simply looking for somewhere to settle down and live in peace. They did not want to get rid of Roman laws and culture. Instead, they tried to blend these into their own way of life. During the long years of struggle, much of the Roman way of life had broken down. Theatres, baths, temples, and aqueducts had been neglected, and left to crumble away. But wherever the barbarians settled they found, firmly based on the ruins of Roman culture, the laws and culture of the Christian Church. All the barbarians except Attila's Huns became Christians. The Church succeeded in tying the rough cloth of the barbarian way of life to the smooth silk of Roman civilization.

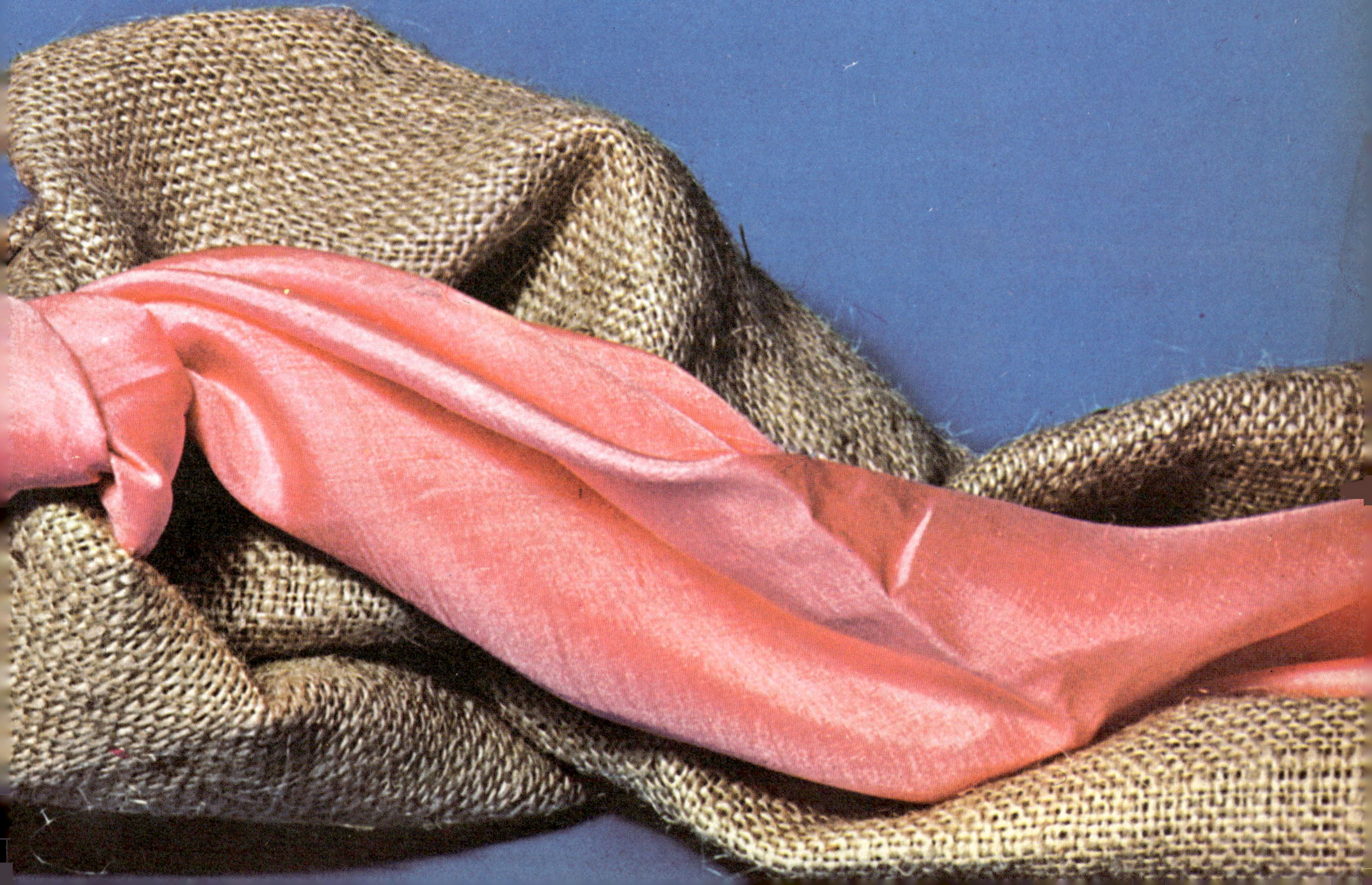

Barbarian art

One of the skills the barbarians carried about with them was their own kind of art. This was quite different from the art of the Greeks and the Romans. Roman art, in particular, was very realistic. Roman artists were especially good at making portraits, or likenesses of people. The people they carved or painted look very much like the people we might see today in the street or on television.

Barbarian artists liked to cover everything they made with patterns. They did not like to see bare, plain surfaces. Their patterns, or designs, were mostly made in metal. The way they are made is called cloisonné, which means ridged. Barbarian artists laid strips of metal, usually of gold, on to a metal background. In the spaces between the metal outlines they put coloured enamels (like hard paint), semi-precious stones, or pieces of coloured glass. All kinds of jewellery and ornaments were made in this way. Some of the designs were based on animals, but the artists did not try to make them look like the living animals. They were interested only in the overall design. Later on, monks in monasteries made handwritten books and painted lovely, ornamental designs in them. These designs were often copied from the patterns on barbarian jewellery.

Justinian and Theodora

This is a picture of the Emperor Justinian, who was the greatest ruler of the Byzantine empire. He was born the son of a poor peasant in Illyria (now Yugoslavia). The story of how he came to the throne is strange. Justinian had an uncle called Justin, who was also a poor peasant. Justin was illiterate, which means that he could not read or write very well. He became a soldier, and rose to be a commander in the bodyguard of the Emperor Anastasius. When Anastasius died, the army made Justin emperor in his place. Justin had no children, so he adopted his nephew and had him educated at Constantinople.

Justinian was very clever, and when he had finished his education he joined his uncle as ruler of the empire. When Justin died, Justinian became the emperor. He was a tireless worker. Long after his subjects were asleep, he roamed the corridors of his palace, thinking and planning. He waged many wars. Italy had become a Gothic kingdom, ruled from the city of Ravenna. Justinian fought the Goths and won Ravenna and the north of Italy. Today he is best remembered for his great books of laws. These laws, called the Justinian Codes, were based on old Roman laws, and are still important in many countries today.

Almost as strange as the story of Justinian the Great is the story of his wife, the Empress Theodora. She was the daughter of a bear-keeper on the island of Cyprus, and was a wandering actress and dancer. Then she married Justinian, and on Justin's death the two were crowned together. Theodora was wise, and kind to the poor. At one time, when there were dreadful riots, or rebellions, in Constantinople, she saved the day by refusing to flee to safety or surrender to the mobs.

The reign of Justinian and Theodora was a great age. Fair and just laws were established. The empire was strengthened. Trade and art blossomed. Wonderful churches were built, and decorated with mosaics. The mosaic opposite of Justinian is in the church of San Vitale in Ravenna. It is different from Roman mosaics, which were made of little pieces of marble. Byzantine artists used tiny cubes of brightly coloured glass, all set at slightly different angles. When the light plays across the surface of these mosaics, the glass glows and sparkles brilliantly.

Constantinople

Less than three years after Justinian died, Germanic barbarians called Lombards swept across Italy. Except for Rome and Ravenna, little was left to the Byzantine empire. To the east, the empire was attacked by Slavs, barbarians from Russia. In the south-east, there was the threat of the Persians. Although it was surrounded by enemies, Constantinople did not fall till much later. This rich and beautiful city was protected as successfully as a bag of grain surrounded by chicken wire.

Trade made Constantinople rich, especially the silk trade. For hundreds of years the Chinese had guarded the secret of silk making, then Justinian sent two monks as Christian messengers to China. The monks found some silkworm eggs, which they hid in the hollow handles of the sticks they carried. In this way they carried the eggs back to Constantinople. The worms were hatched and the Byzantines could then make and sell silk. They also traded in furs from Russia, and in perfumes, spices, and ivory from the east. They had guilds that looked after the trades, and they made rules about what people were allowed to do and to sell.

Religion was an important part of life in Constantinople. The emperor claimed to represent God on earth. This claim was challenged, and the challenge came from Rome.

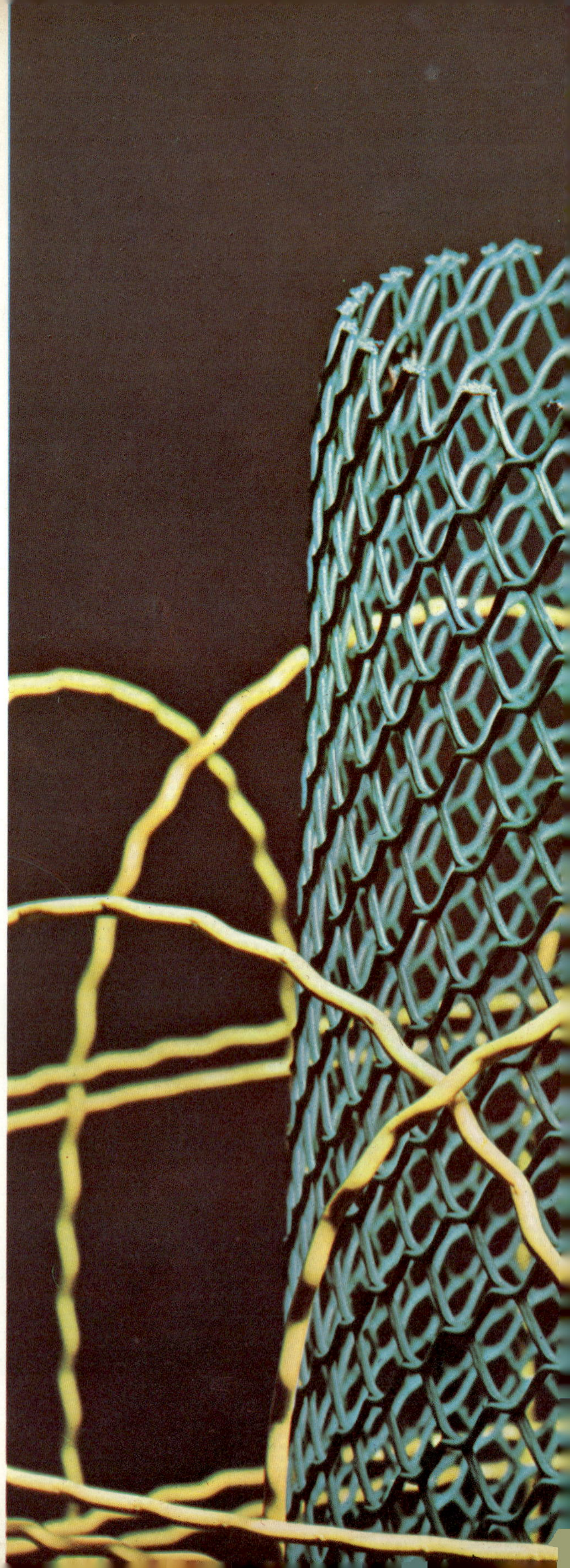

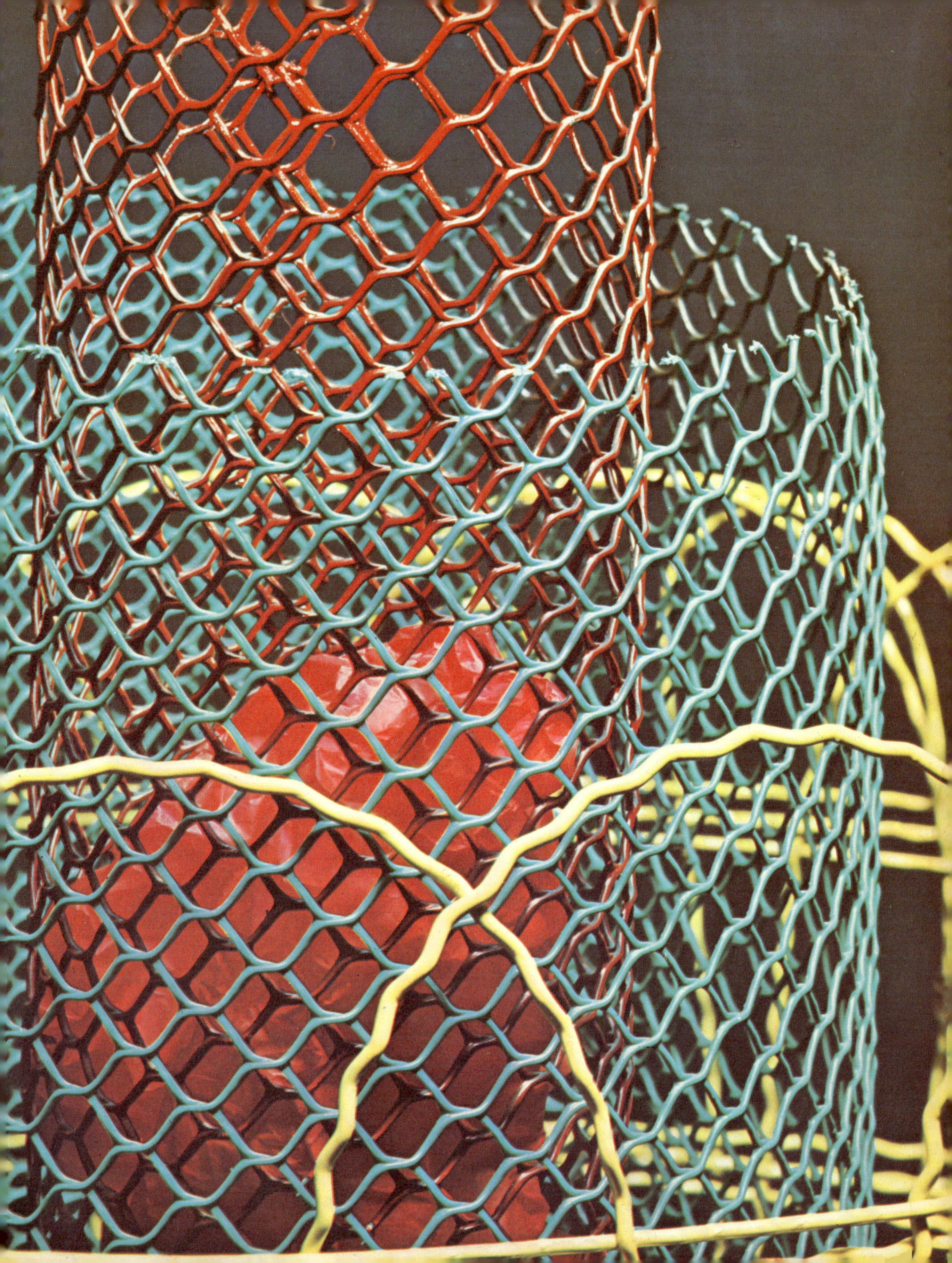

The Bishop of Rome

Constantine had moved his capital from west to east because Byzantium was a safer place than Rome. As a small Greek city, it had already existed for about 900 years. Placed at the eastern edge of Europe, and built on rising ground, it was easier to defend than Rome. Also, its position between the Mediterranean and the Black Sea was good for trade. But it was not the same kind of city as Rome. Its laws were Roman, but its language was Greek. Surrounded by enemies, gradually it lost contact with the Latin-speaking world. Its buildings were a mixture of classical columns (Greek), arches (Roman), and domes (from Persia and the East). Its religion was a mixture of Hellenistic philosophy and Christianity.

Christians in Rome began to feel they had little in common with Christians in Constantinople, most of whom did not even speak the same language. In particular, they did not want the leader of their church to be the emperor of a far off city. The bishops of the church were appointed by the emperor. To him, the Bishop of Rome was no more important than any of his other bishops. The Romans felt differently. Various sects, or parts, of the church were busy arguing among themselves as to which ideas about God were right, and which were wrong. Meanwhile, the church itself slowly divided into two main groups. The eastern group still accepted the emperor as leader of their faith. This group was to grow into the eastern Orthodox church of today. The leader of the western group was the Bishop of Rome. Later, he was called pope, which means father.

Torches in the night

The period in European history that followed the end of the Roman empire is known as the Middle Ages. It lasted about one thousand years and is the bridge between the ancient and the modern world. The early part of this time is often called the Dark Ages, as though the light of civilization no longer shone in western Europe. This was only partly true. The Christian monasteries, like torches glowing in the darkness of night, kept the flame of learning alight.

People lived mainly in small communities, like villages, and the monastery was the centre of each community. Often the priests and monks were the only people in the village who could read and write. A monastery was not just one building but a whole group of buildings. There would be a church, sleeping quarters, a hospital, workshops, gardens, and orchards. Monasteries were strongly built to withstand attack and give shelter to frightened people. The Dark Ages was a time of fear, robbery, and violence.

The most famous monk of the time was Gregory, who became Pope Gregory I, the Great. The lovely hymns he wrote, called Gregorian chants, are still sung in churches throughout the world today.

Baltic Sea
North Sea
Angles
Saxons
Slavs
Saxons
Franks
Lombards
Ostrogoths
Mediterranean Sea

The pope gives a crown

Pope Gregory I was anxious to bring all those people who were still pagan, or not Christian, into the Christian church. He sent a party of forty monks to Britain, under the leadership of a monk called Augustine. Gregory gave Augustine careful instructions about what he was to do in Britain. In fact, his orders were of little use. The twenty-four Roman cities in Britain he knew about no longer existed. Many of them had been burned down. The people were pagans, speaking a Germanic language. There were Christians in Britain, the Celts, but they were the enemies of the southern Angles and Saxons. Augustine was treated well by

Ethelbert, king of Kent. The king himself was a convert to Christianity, as were many of his subjects.

Augustine baptized, or received into the church, 10,000 people in one day. The pope made him the first Archbishop of Canterbury.

Although the Christian faith grew stronger, this did not end the troubles of the popes. Quarrels with the emperor of the East and his bishops grew more bitter. The popes needed help, and they turned to the rulers of the Franks (or French) who had long been Christian. The Franks had kings, but they were weak. The people were really ruled by the Mayors of the Palace. One of these mayors, Pepin, agreed to support the pope. In return, the pope

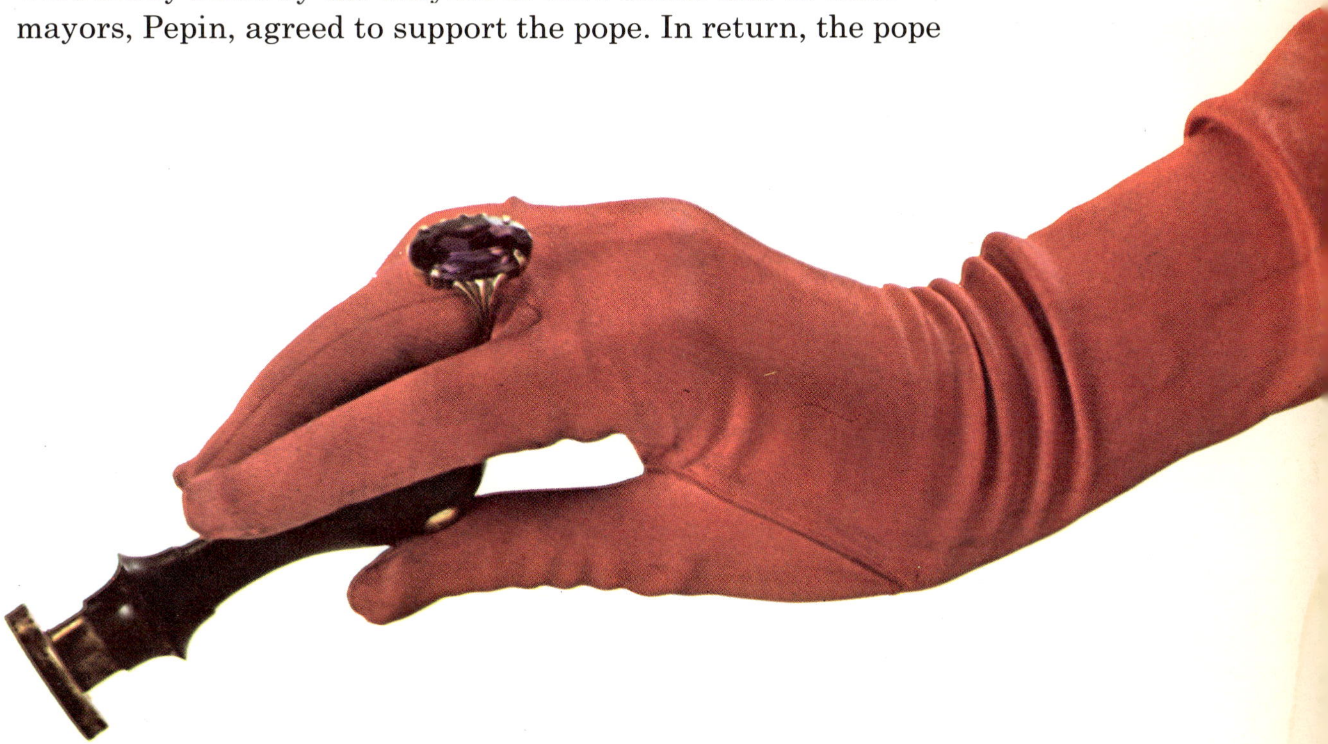

helped him to overthrow the king and take his place. This was the beginning of a friendship between church and state that turned the Frankish Kingdom into the Holy Roman Empire. Fifty years later, another pope crowned Pepin's son, Charlemagne, as the first emperor.

The rise of Islam

Mohammed

Not very long before Augustine set out on his mission to Britain, a son was born to a poor merchant in the town of Mecca, in Arabia. While the child was still young, both his mother and father died. The little boy, Mohammed, was left an orphan at only six years old. He was looked after by his grandfather, and later by his uncle. Through the city of Mecca, where he lived, ran an important main road. Many caravans, or groups of merchants and travellers, passed along this road. For a time the boy, Mohammed, earned money guarding sheep. Then he became a camel driver on the caravan route. When he was twenty-four he went to work as a merchant for a woman called Khadija. Mohammed and Khadija married, were very happy, and had two sons and four daughters.

Mohammed worked as a merchant for the next fifteen years. But he spent more and more of his time thinking about God. At that time there were both Judaism (the Jewish religion) and some Christianity in Arabia. Mohammed believed in God. He thought of Jesus as a prophet, or someone who understood God's teaching. He did not agree with Judaism or with the Christians. One day, at a mountain near Mecca, he fell into a trance or dream. The angel Gabriel appeared to him in this trance and told him to preach the true religion. Many people in Mecca were angry when Mohammed started to preach. He had to escape to another town, Medina. There, he and his faithful followers built their first mosque, or temple. The year in which Mohammed fled from Mecca was 622 AD. The Arabs call this year *Hegira*, meaning flight. It is a very important date and time. Just as Christians begin their calendar at the time of Jesus' birth, so Mohammedans begin their calendar and reckoning of time at the Hegira.

Mohammed called his new religion Islam, which means submission. Its followers are called Moslems. Mohammed called them to the mosque to worship Allah (God) five times every day. He taught them to treat each other kindly, to be good to slaves and animals, to drink no wine, and to worship no idols. In return he promised they would live forever in Allah's Garden, Paradise.

The prince of Arabia

Mohammed's preaching had so angered the people that when he fled from Mecca he was in danger of being killed. There is an Islamic legend (a story) that he had to escape from a band of Arabs who did not believe in his new religion. The legend tells that he hid in a cave, where Allah sent him a huge spider to spin a web over the entrance. The web protected Mohammed from his attackers.

When he reached Medina he was appointed judge, ruler of the city and of two powerful tribes. He began to teach about his new religion, and found many more followers. When he had enough followers to support him, he turned warrior against the enemies of Islam. He fought his first battle with the people of Mecca.

After a struggle lasting several years, Mohammed conquered Mecca. He was accepted as chief and prophet, and Islam became the religion of Arabia. People flocked from all parts of the country to recognize Mohammed as Allah's prophet, and as prince of Arabia. He had come not only as a religious leader, but as ruler of the first Moslem state.

Mohammed was not content with that. He wanted to convert the rest of the world to Islam. Just before he died, he prepared his people to go to war with Syria, which was a part of the Byzantine empire. After his death, his plans were carried out.

The Koran

Mohammed had a number of trances in which the angel Gabriel appeared and spoke to him, telling him God's word. At first, Mohammed told no one except his wife, children, and one friend, about these dreams. Later, he told his followers. Although Mohammed himself could not read or write, his followers wrote down all that the angel had said to him. After Mohammed's death the collected sayings were put together in a book. This book is called the Koran. It is the Mohammedan bible.

The Koran is written in rhyming prose—it is not poetry, although many of the words rhyme as they do in poetry. Mohammed said that these sayings were Allah's words to the Arabs in their own tongue. He believed that Allah had also spoken to the Jews and the Christians in their own languages and through their own prophets. Like Jesus, he taught his followers to love one another, to worship the one true God, and not to worship idols (pictures and statues).

The Koran teaches that the task of Moslems is to spread Islam through the world. At the same time, the Moslem is told to respect religions like Christianity and Judaism, which also have holy scriptures or writings. When Mohammed's followers went on to conquer Syria and Egypt, they did not persecute the Christians and Jews who lived there.

The holy city

One of the laws Mohammed made was that Moslems must turn towards the holy city of Mecca each time they pray. If you look at a compass you will see that the needle always points north.

In a way Moslems behave like a compass needle. Wherever they are, five times a day, they turn towards Mecca to pray. Today, there are about 400,000,000 (400 million) Moslems all over the world.

LUNA PARK

Heaven and hell

Mohammed taught that those who obeyed the word of Allah would live forever in Heaven or Paradise. This was good news for his followers. Most of Arabia is hot, dry desert. Little will grow there, and people could not settle and farm the land. Instead they had to roam about, finding a living as best they could. They liked to think that things would be better after they died.

Mohammed said the angel Gabriel had shown him Paradise in a vision. He said it was an enormous garden, full of green meadows and shady trees. Everything that anyone wanted could be found there. Even children would be happy. For them, it would be like a huge fairground. To reach Paradise, Moslems had to carry out the religious duties Mohammed preached which were: recite five daily prayers; fast or eat only certain kinds of food during the month called Ramadan; pay the poor tax; make a pilgrimage or holy journey to Mecca once in their lifetime. For those who obeyed these rules, the gates of Paradise would be opened. They would open to soldiers too who died in battle with the infidels (non-Moslems). Wars and soldiers were important to the Moslems, for they hoped to conquer the world in the name of their faith. One of the symbols of Islam was the double sword.

Mohammed also said that the angel Gabriel had shown him a vision of Hell. It was a terrifying place of boiling oil, fire, and demons. Those who did not obey Allah, said Mohammed, would burn in Hell forever.

The crimson crescent

When Mohammed died, someone had to take charge of the Islamic people. The man chosen, Abu Bakr, was not a prophet. He was simply a leader or ruler. He was called the caliph, which means the successor. All the leaders who came after him were also known as caliphs. The first caliphs were strong leaders. With their armies of wild Bedouin tribesmen from the Arabian desert, they conquered many lands. Syria, Egypt, Persia, and much of North Africa fell to Islam. So the Moslem empire grew.

But weak caliphs led to quarrels within the empire. At last, there came to be two main families of caliphs, the Umayyads and the Abbasids. Their followers formed two sects which still exist to this day.

Having won much of North Africa, it was easy for the Moslem armies to cross the narrow Strait of Gibraltar into Spain. They defeated the Goths, who had lived there for 300 years, and set up a kingdom stretching as far north as the Pyrenees Mountains. Meanwhile, in the east, they were attacking Constantinople. This Arabic-speaking empire was ruled by the Umayyads, who wanted to go on and conquer the whole of Europe. Exactly one hundred years after Mohammed's death, their troops rode northwards across the Pyrenees. They reached Central France, but there they were stopped by an army of Christian Franks. Defeated at the battle of Poitiers, they were forced to retreat towards Spain. The Frankish leader was Charles Martel, father of Pepin who was to form an alliance with the pope. Because of him, Europe became a Christian continent, instead of Islamic.

The Umayyad caliphs ruled their empire from Damascus, in Syria. After a rebellion, the Abbasids became caliphs and moved their capital to Baghdad. Here a great culture grew up, based on the Hellenistic culture which had lasted since the days of Alexander. Under the Abbasids, the Islamic empire included, as well as North Africa, Spain, parts of Italy, Crete, Sicily, and parts of India. It was not a united empire, for the Umayyads still ruled Spain. The crimson crescent, the symbol of Islam, had many cracks in it. Slowly, the great empire broke up, but its religion and much of its culture are still with us today.

Islamic art

We often admire the wonderful designs on Oriental (eastern) carpets. It is said that these designs developed as they did largely because of Mohammed's teaching. The Koran forbids the making of images (pictures), so the Mohammedans drew patterns instead. The beautiful, curving, lace-like shapes they made, often based on flowers, are called arabesques. They were painted in books, on walls, and woven into silks and carpets. Later, Mohammedans were allowed to paint people as long as they had nothing to do with religion, but still the pictures were lacy and patterned. Even Arabic script looks like a pattern, and their writing is often used in designs.

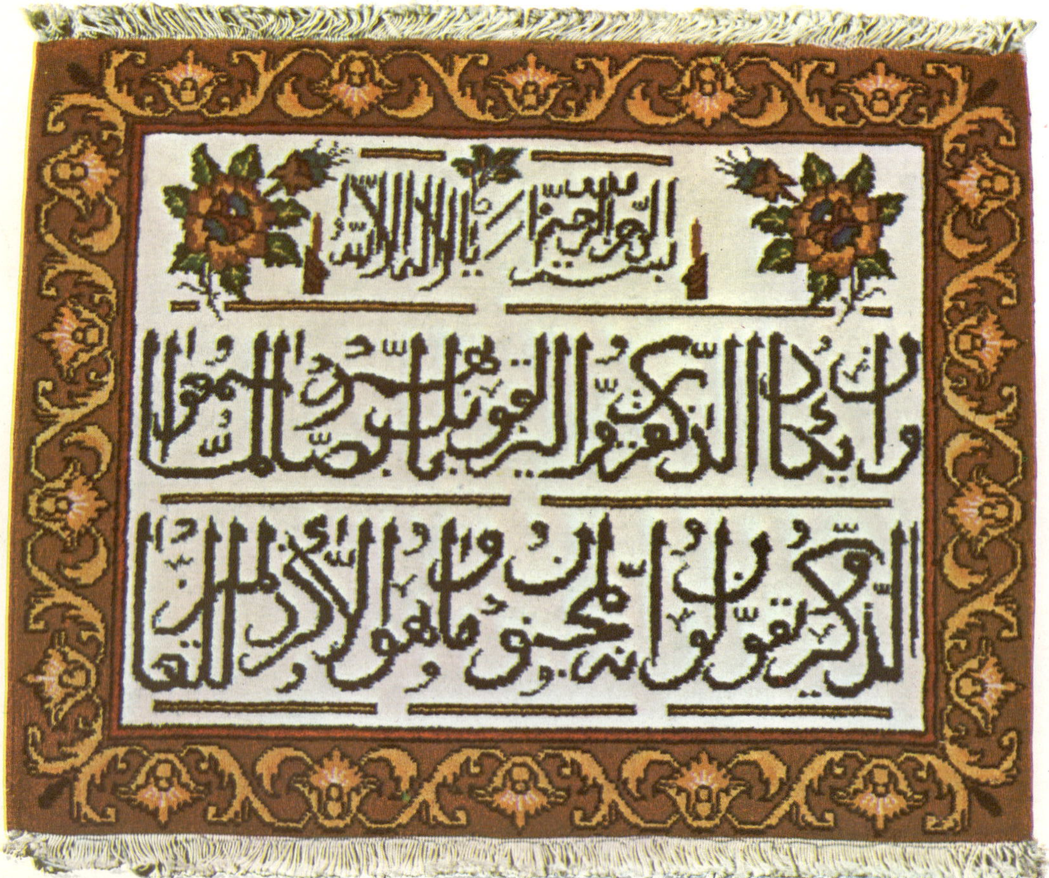

123 456
1
123456
123

The learning of Islam

During the Dark Ages in western Europe, when the only learning was in the monasteries, the Arabs had great schools, universities, and libraries. The Abbasid caliphs set up a postal service to keep them in touch with all parts of the empire. Pilgrimages to Mecca meant that people travelled, met each other, and talked about their ideas. Trade routes to India, China, and Ceylon (now Sri Lanka), as well as to the Mediterranean, were opened. The caliphs and their people grew rich, and could afford to pay artists and scientists. Medicine, astronomy, and mathematics were studied. Books were written. Splendid mosques and palaces were built. Fine dishes of pottery, glass, and carved crystal were made.

The learning of the Arabs affects our lives to this day. Many Arabic words have become part of our language. Alcohol, algebra, coffee, magazine, talc, traffic, and zero are only a few of them. The Arabs invented algebra. They also gave us the numerals we use: 0, 1, 2, 3, 4, 5, 6, 7, 8, 9, 10. Roman numerals, I, II, III, IV, V, were much harder to use. The Arabs were quick to learn from the people they traded with or conquered. They really found the numerals in India, and improved them. In the same way, they found out how to make paper from the Chinese, and so they learned how to produce books.

Magical "science"

Chemistry in the Middle Ages was a strange mixture of science and magic. It was called alchemy, which is an Arabic word. The men who practised it were called alchemists. Most alchemists spent their time trying to find the Philosopher's Stone. They believed there were two kinds of Philosopher's Stone. One was white and would turn ordinary metals into silver. The other was red and would turn them into gold. Their search was mixed up with astrology, or belief in the powers of the stars and planets. Some stars and planets were supposed to affect certain metals, and to reflect them in the heavens. The sun was thought to reflect gold, the moon silver, the planet Mars iron, and so on.

Alchemists worked in secret. They ground all kinds of substances into powders, burned the powders to produce gases, and melted metals in their furnaces. There was little real science in what they did. They were simply experimenting to see what happened. When things did happen, the alchemists often did not know why. They thought magic powers were at work. It is easy to laugh at them now, but they lived in an age of ignorance, and ignorance leads to superstition or belief in magic. People believed in ghosts and demons, and wore charms to keep them away. They thought some things were lucky and some were unlucky. All the things they did not understand frightened them.

Life in the Middle Ages was harsh, and often short. Mysterious disease could suddenly kill a whole community. No one would know what caused it or how to cure it. For hundreds of years, the Christian Church would not allow men to study medicine. It was thought to be a pagan science. The Church forbade doctors to dissect bodies in order to find out how they worked. Only the Arabs could preserve and add to the medical knowledge of the ancient world. It is not surprising that people turned to magic, and hoped the alchemists would discover the Elixir of Life. Elixir is also an Arabic word. The Elixir of Life was a magic medicine that would help people to live forever. As we all know, the alchemists failed in their search for everlasting life.

The Norsemen

Land of Thule

Three hundred years before the birth of Jesus, a Greek called Pytheas sailed to a land called Thule, six days north of the Shetland Isles. Thule was probably Norway. Certainly, both the Greeks and Romans knew people lived in the far north of Europe. The Romans even traded with some of them. There were people in the land we call Czechoslovakia who acted as dealers, passing Roman goods to the north, and northern furs, skins, and seal skin ropes to the Romans.

In those early times in Scandinavia, there were no towns, no stone buildings, and no books. People lived in houses made of wattle and daub (twigs plastered with mud or clay). The roof rested on wooden posts, and had a hole in it to allow the smoke from the fire to escape. Inside was just one big room, where men, women, children, and animals huddled together for warmth. Life in winter must have been hard. We know these early Scandinavians grew grain, and made bread. A small bread roll, about 1,500 years old, has actually been found in Sweden. Sheep, goats, and cattle provided clothes, milk, and meat. Only the strong animals could survive the hard winters, so the weaker ones were killed, and the meat was smoked or salted to preserve it for food.

The Norsemen, or Vikings, of Scandinavia were farmers, and they were also sailors, traders, and shipbuilders. Their own lands did not provide a good living, but sea-trading and pirating did. Vikings were bold people who loved fighting, feasting, and singing. In spite of the fact that they lived in small, separate states and often fought each other, all the Norsemen had the same gods. The two most important were Thor, the God of Thunder, and Odin, the Lord of War and inventor of song. Heroes killed in war were taken to Odin's paradise, Valhalla. There they could fight, feast, and sing till the end of time.

Viking ships...in life and death

Viking is the name by which the early peoples of the far north were known. The sea was important to the Vikings, so they learned to build fast, seaworthy ships. If we still had to build wooden ships today, we could scarcely build them better. Many Viking ships were clinker-built, with planks overlapping downwards. They were long and open, with a single sail and many pairs of oars. The Viking pirates used them as floating machines for scooping up wealth. They even carried carts aboard, to be loaded up with stolen goods.

Because the sea was so important in the life of the Vikings, it was also important in death. They had a legend about the mystical ship of death, which carried the souls of the dead far away across the oceans. It was therefore reasonable that they should bury people in ships. Most of these disappeared without trace. Some sank into waterlogged clay, which preserved them for many hundreds of years. The beautiful ship opposite was dug up at a place called Oseburg. A princess was buried in it, with an attendant and a number of dogs, horses, and oxen. There were also a cart, four sledges, beds, a chest, buckets, and many everyday articles.

FREYRIE
FREYRIE
SIDERAL

Robbers on skis

The Vikings were always looking for countries they could invade and rob. They found it was not easy to raid the lands to the south, where the Franks and the Saxons were strong. To the east and west, on the other hand, the way was open and the countries almost undefended.

Swedish Vikings journeyed east, into the land of the Slavs, which we now know as Russia. Crossing the great snow-covered plains would be no problem for these men from the north, who were used to cold conditions at home. We know that they had developed skis, simpler than those we have today but not unlike them. They probably used the skis to hunt, to give them greater speed. No doubt they made good use of their skiing ability when finding their way across the icy wastes of Russia.

The Swedes settled among the Slavs, who accepted their rule. Then they looked towards Constantinople, envying its riches and its civilization. Four times the Viking fleets attacked the city, and four times they were beaten back. In the end, Swedish soldiers joined the emperor's bodyguard and actually helped to defend Constantinople. Thanks to the Vikings, the culture and religion of the Byzantine world slowly spread into Russia.

The Danelaw

While the Swedes were forcing their way into Russia, the Danes and the Norwegians turned westwards. The Danes, being nearer the English Channel, threw themselves on Frisia (Holland), England, and France. The Norwegians attacked the Orkneys, Shetland, the Hebrides, northern Scotland, Northumbria, the Isle of Man, and Ireland. The Vikings soon discovered that the monasteries were the richest places, and made them the main target of their attacks. The Irish monasteries in particular, were crammed with treasure. Once the Vikings had set eyes on their gold and silver ornaments, rich brocades, and precious stones, they could not leave them alone. For the Vikings, these raids were a kind of enjoyable game. After the gloom and boredom of a long, northern winter, it was fun to set sail on the first breeze of summer. They enjoyed a good raid just as we might enjoy a good trip to the seaside.

In England, the Vikings fought and won many fierce battles. Then they began to settle in districts of their own, with their own kings. One area they did not win was the kingdom of Wessex, in the south west. This was ruled by Alfred the Great, a very wise man. Alfred was only twenty-three when he became king, but he was clever and brave. He raised an army and marched on the dreaded Vikings. Not only did he keep them out of Wessex, he drove them back to the east.

A treaty, or agreement, was drawn up allowing them to keep their strip of eastern England, called the Danelaw. Today, we can still see signs of the Danelaw in the strangely carved stones the Vikings left behind. They are known as runic stones, and the odd looking letters on the stones are called runes.

Rulers of the sea

Invasion followed invasion, till it seemed that the sea swarmed with terrifying Vikings in their horned helmets. After the Danelaw in England came another Danelaw in Normandy, France. In Iceland the Vikings set up the first real parliament since the time of the Greeks. Laws were made by an assembly, or meeting of all the landowners on the island. This type of parliament still exists on the Isle of Man, which was an old Viking colony. It meets every year, on Midsummers day.

The Vikings even sailed as far as America. A famous Viking leader, Leif Ericsson, is said to have discovered the continent by accident, when his ship was blown off course by strong winds. The ship was blown all the way to the land we now call Labrador. There Leif Ericsson stayed for several months, until he had repaired his ship and he could sail home again. Later, a small Viking fleet reached North America. The Vikings went ashore and started to farm the land, but they were attacked again and again by American Indians. At last a single ship returned to the Scandinavian homeland with only a few survivors on board.

A Viking empire

For many years, King Alfred the Great and his successors ruled that part of Britain from the Channel to the River Clyde. Then a weak king came to the throne. He was called Ethelred. His nickname was Ethelred the Unready. The Vikings knew he could not hold them in the Danelaw. Once again, they started to make ferocious attacks on all parts of the country.

Ethelred's government tried to buy off the Vikings. They introduced a tax called Danegeld. Most people could not afford to pay much money. They became poorer, and the Danes became richer. It did not stop them from conquering Britain. They won more and more of the country, until Ethelred had to flee and Britain became a Viking land, ruled by Danish kings.

The most famous of these Danish kings was Canute. Under his rule, Britain became part of the Viking Empire which stretched all the way from the north of Norway to Cornwall. The Vikings also held part of France. When they invaded France the Frankish people called them Normans, meaning men from the North. The land where they settled is called Normandy to this day. Both Normandy and England were rich countries. The poor pirates who had come to rob them, no longer had any need to steal from other people, for they were rich themselves.

A mixture of peoples

If you pour two liquids of different colours into a glass, three things may happen. The liquids may not mix together, so that you can still see both colours. Or the liquids may mix perfectly, forming a third colour. Or one colour may be stronger than the other and may absorb or swallow up the other colour. The same three things can happen when two different peoples come together. In the case of the Vikings, they were completely absorbed by the French.

France was too strong for the Vikings to take over. French civilization survived, and the Vikings admired and imitated it. They became Christians, and started to speak French. Each area of France was called a duchy, which means that each one was ruled by a duke. Soon Normandy was simply another French duchy. The Normans invaded and conquered England in the year 1066. They brought their own laws and customs with them. These laws and customs were not Viking ones, but French.

Old empires and new

Empires can be compared with candles. Although each can glow with a brilliant flame, each can also burn away. Byzantium burned away, its flame growing slowly dimmer. Islam burned too fiercely and too fast. Both empires had lost their brilliance, but they left Europe locked in a struggle between different religions. Islam held one shore of the Mediterranean, Christianity the other. As a result, trade suffered. Seaports that were once rich were almost abandoned, and left to fall into ruin. Even Christianity was split between Byzantium in the east and Rome in the west.

No power in Europe seemed to be strong enough to form a new empire to replace the old ones. We have spoken of France, but in fact France as we know it did not exist in the eighth century. Nor did any of the other present-day countries.

There was a king of the western Franks, but no France. There was a king of the eastern Franks, but no Germany. There was a king of the Lombards, but no Italy. There was no great civilization to replace that of the old empires . . . no great art or architecture, no great books or poems or music.

In fact, there was a new empire to come. Like a candle, it was only waiting for someone to set it alight. The empire was the Holy Roman Empire. The man who was to set it alight was Charlemagne, son of Pepin.

Charlemagne

Hero of the Dark Ages

The name Charlemagne means Charles the Great. On Pepin's death, Charles and his brother Carloman shared the throne. Then Carloman died, and Charles was the sole ruler. Pepin had given Charles good advice. He had told him to support the Church, and defend it against its enemies; to fight the heathen (non-Christian) Lombards and Moslems; and to improve the government. Charles always followed his father's advice.

The Lombards, in Italy, were giving the pope trouble. Charles tried to sort things out peacefully. When this failed to work, he fought the Lombards, and made himself their king. He gave the pope authority over a part of Central Italy. This area became the Papal state. The pope still rules it, after more than 1,000 years.

Having solved the problem of the Lombards, Charles turned his attention to the Saxons and to the Avars, who lived along the River Danube. The Avars were wiped out; the Saxons defeated and converted to Christianity. Charles also marched against the Moors, or Moslems, in Spain, and won some victories.

The pope now felt that he needed a strongly ruled empire to support him, but popes had enemies who challenged their authority. Pope Leo III was actually attacked and beaten up in the streets of Rome. There was no one with enough power to protect the pope and support the Church. An emperor was needed and only one man was suitable. In the year 800, Charles was crowned emperor of the new Holy Roman Empire by Leo III.

Charles was worthy of his great position. He was bold yet kindly, stern yet popular. To his Frankish warriors he was the ideal chief. In looks he was tall and stout, with flashing blue eyes. A mighty hunter, he loved the Frankish speech and the old Frankish songs. He even wore the traditional costume—high laced boots, scarlet hose or stockings, with crossed garters, linen tunic and square mantle or cape of white or blue. Although he was a hearty man who enjoyed life, he was simple in his needs and sparing in food and drink.

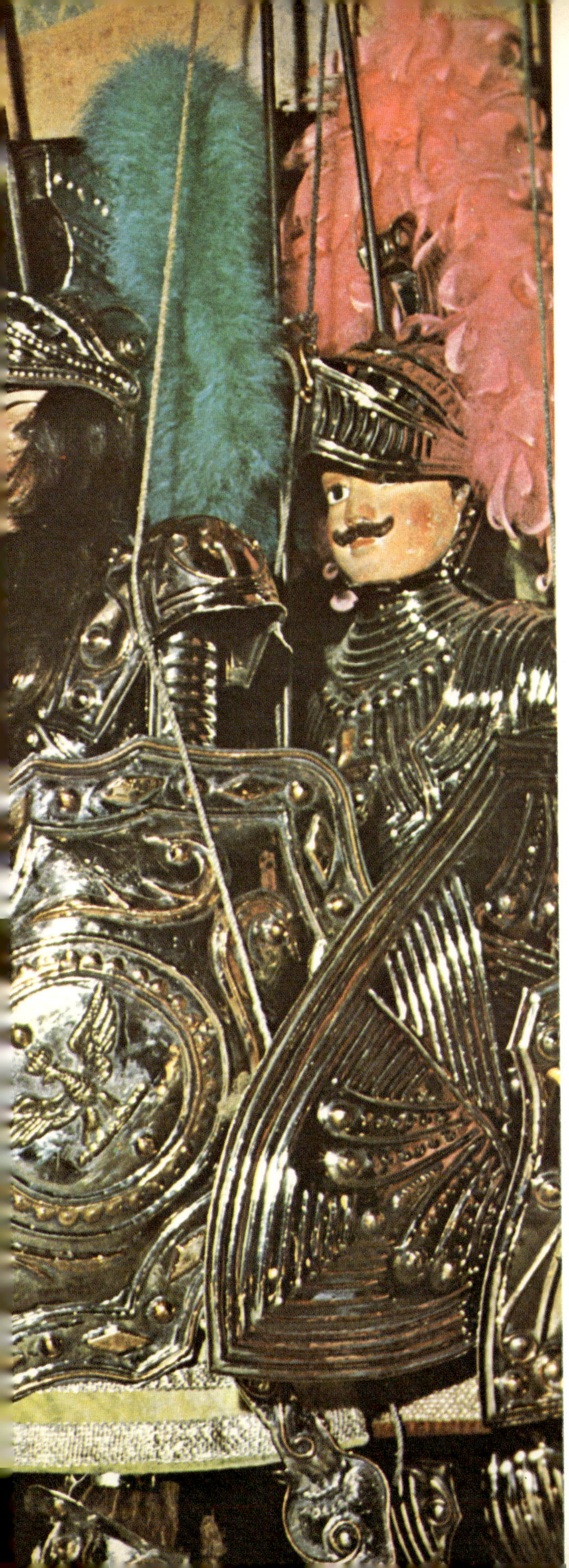

The paladins

Charlemagne's most trusted knights, or warriors, lived with him in his palace. The Latin word for a palace is *palatium*, so the knights who lived in the palace are known as paladins. In all twelve paladins lived in Charlemagne's household.

Charlemagne's paladins followed him everywhere. At home they formed his guard of honour. When he went off to war they were the captains of his soldiers. They were so brave and bold that many legends grew up about them, telling of their wonderful deeds and their adventures.

Moslems who fought against Christians were known as Saracens. As Charlemagne's struggles with the Saracens became more fierce the more heroic became the stories told about his glorious paladins. Songs were sung about them and one of the best known was *Chanson de Roland*. This very early ballad was also sung by wandering minstrels, or musicians, and by the performers who entertained the rich in the great houses. According to legend, Roland, the hero of the song, was supposed to be the nephew of Charlemagne. Later, the crusaders sang it as they journeyed to Palestine. Today, traditional puppet shows in Sicily still tell the story of Charlemagne's paladins.

Knowledge flowers

Charlemagne himself was not an educated man, but he believed in the importance of learning. He brought many wise men to his court, and started a school for poor children. The manuscript (handwritten) books of this time, and the beautiful pictures painted in them, are known as Carolingian. This simply means that they belong to the time of Charles.

Although Charlemagne believed in learning, this does not mean he was a solemn man. In fact, he loved to play jokes, particularly if he thought people deserved to be made to look a little silly. There is a story that he once came across a group of noblemen dressed in very splendid clothes, with long robes and curling feathers in their hats. Charlemagne asked them to hunt with him. He was their emperor so they could not refuse. Their fine clothes must have looked very bedraggled after a long ride through forests and undergrowth.

Charlemagne appointed Alcuin, the master of a monastic school at York, to be the controller of education for the Holy Roman Empire. Alcuin was delighted with his task, and worked very hard at it, but he could not work miracles. Europe was still illiterate (the people could not read), and there was little scientific thought. But, like the first blossoms of spring after a long, hard winter, an interest in learning appeared again.

The Holy Roman Empire

The new empire was well-named. It stretched from the Mediterranean Sea to the North Sea and the Baltic, from the River Oder in the east to the Rhône River in the west. The heart of the empire was the country we call Germany. Within these wide boundaries lived all those Christians who supported the pope as the head of the Christian religion.

Charlemagne made this safe empire for the Christian Church. He travelled from village to village, asking questions and solving problems. With his support, great abbeys rose up.

Although Charlemagne's rule was wise and Christian, life was still harsh for many of his subjects. People suspected of committing crimes were not tried in a court of law and given a chance to defend themselves. Instead, they had to stand trial by ordeal. The ordeal was some form of torture, such as branding with red-hot irons. People believed that the innocent were not harmed by these ordeals. And they thought that those who died as a result of their torture must be guilty.

The important thing about the Holy Roman empire was not its cruelty, but its unity. Since Roman times the peoples of Europe had lived side-by-side but apart, like the separate grains of sugar in a bowl. Charlemagne melted and spun the grains together to form one great mass—a great Christian empire.

A broken jigsaw

The law of the Franks said that a man's property had to be divided up among his sons when he died. The Holy Roman Empire was Charlemagne's property. When he died, it was divided among his sons. But an empire cannot be ruled by several different people at once. Nor can it be ruled by one man, unless he is exceptionally wise and strong.

Charlemagne's sons were not wise and strong. The empire was like a difficult jigsaw puzzle, which Charlemagne had pieced together carefully, bit by bit. On his death, his sons pulled it apart into separate little pieces again. Each of them treated his own kingdom as a private estate, to be divided up yet again among his own sons.

When an empire starts to fall apart wars usually break out. In the years following Charlemagne's death, many wars broke out. Once again, different peoples refused to live together peacefully. In Germany, even the tribes of the same race, the Saxons, quarrelled among themselves.

The popes tried hard to re-unite the empire by bringing it back under the rule of one man. The man chosen to be crowned, Charles the Fat, was a descendant of Charlemagne. He was not a success. He was put off the throne, and there were no more Carolingian emperors.

The winds of change

Under the cabbage leaves

Long ago, people used to tell a story about babies being born under cabbage leaves. If we were to think of modern Europe as a baby, its birthday would be about 1,000 years ago, and the cabbage that sheltered it would be the Christian Church.

The breaking up of Charlemagne's empire had one important result. The way in which it was broken up led to the birth of the nations of Western Europe, as we know them today.

In spite of the wars and confusion, the idea of a Christian empire did not die. One hundred and forty-eight years after Charlemagne's death, the pope crowned Otto, son of the first king of Germany, as Holy Roman Emperor. His empire was not the same as Charlemagne's. Otto had already made himself ruler of Hungary and Italy, but his empire was really a German empire. He had proved himself to be a powerful ruler, so no one objected to his new empire. In fact, the Holy Roman Empire of the German nation lasted right up to the nineteenth century.

The rule of the Holy Roman Empire did not affect all of Europe. Other countries went on developing in their own way, though still within the Christian Church.

Homes and fortresses

During the early Middle Ages, people lived in villages, with little protection from raiding enemies. The poor found shelter from attack within the thick walls of the monasteries. The rich built castles which were really fortresses. Many castles were encircled by a moat, or large ditch full of water.

The drawbridge over the moat could be drawn up whenever an enemy approached. The outer walls of the castles were very thick, and protected by turrets. From the battlements arrows could be shot, and boiling water, tar or lead could be poured on the heads of the enemy. Using giant slings to hurl sharp stones over the walls, the enemy attacked the occupants of castles.

Each large castle was like a small town. In the outer court would be the shops of craftsmen such as blacksmiths, saddlers, tailors, carpenters, and shoemakers. There would be stables for the horses, cows, pigs. Chickens and sometimes smaller animals would wander about the castle interior freely.

Feudalism

Feudalism really began when Charlemagne divided the lands he had conquered into countries, and gave them to the nobles, or vassals. The vassals controlled their own small armies, and watched over the people who worked their lands.

The warriors were all nobles. They were called knights. As well as fighting, they hunted with hounds or falcons, and took part in jousts. These jousts were a kind of mock fight on horseback. Each knight had to try not to kill his opponent but to unseat him from his horse. To help him do this, he was armed with a long lance.

Below the rank of knights came the freemen. They were allowed to farm the land or not, as they chose, as long as they paid taxes to the lord of the manor and served in his army when necessary.

Lower in rank than the freemen were the peasants, who were the property of the lord of the manor, although they could not be bought or sold. They had to farm his land, bake his bread, care for his animals, and do everything else they were asked to do. In return, they were allowed to grow their own food and keep their own animals. But they had to give a part of everything they produced to their overlord. They never had any money. Everything was bought and sold by barter, or exchange of goods.

The crusades

The first crusade was so poor, it was rather like people setting out on bicycles, in an age of motor cars. In spite of this, it was the only really successful crusade. The second one failed to achieve anything. The third was organized by Frederick Barbarossa (Redbeard) of Germany, a great leader. Barbarossa was drowned and the crusade ended, shamefully, in a truce with Saladin, the Saracen leader.

The fourth crusade was captured by the Venetians and turned against Constantinople, like an old-time gangster raid. All the crusades after that ended badly. The worst was the crusade where 30,000 children were led by a twelve-year-old boy. Those who did not die of cold and hunger were captured and sold as slaves. It had seemed a good idea for the Christians to crusade to free the Holy Land from Turkish Moslems who killed visiting pilgrims. But the crusades were not a glorious triumph for Christianity.

Fitting together in towns

In a way, the crusades helped to open up the trade routes between west and east again. For hundreds of years people in the west had lived in small villages. Needs were simple, craftsmen were few and, under the feudal barter system, little money changed hands. As trade increased, people grew richer and wanted to spend money on goods of different kinds.

Villages soon turned into towns as more and more people flocked into them, partly to escape from the rule of the feudal lords. This growth of the towns was the beginning of the end of feudalism. Newly-rich merchants and bankers needed craftsmen to build and repair their houses, make their clothes and shoes, mix their medicines, and fashion fine gold and silverware. To make sure that only skilled people practised the various crafts, the craftsmen formed themselves into guilds. Some of the finest buildings of the time were the guild halls, where the craftsmen

carried out their trade, held meetings, elected officers and paid their membership money.

People no longer lived in quarrelsome tribes. They only needed to be protected from the thieves and criminals among themselves. Nightwatchmen were employed to walk the streets with lanterns, keeping an eye open for suspicious characters and calling out to assure nervous citizens that all was well. Taverns and inns sprang up to serve people with food and drink. Because few people could read, inns usually had colourful pictures as signs. For the same reason, an apothecary or chemist showed a mortar and pestle (a bowl and a spoon-like tool for crushing things). The combined trade of barber and surgeon was shown by a red and white striped pole—red for blood and white for towels.

Towns started to have their own government. A mayor was elected and a town council chosen to make the laws for each town. This government held the town together and made it work, rather like the base of a shape puzzle. It helped all the different kinds of people, like different shapes in the puzzle, to fit into the right place and make a complete object.

Beauty and faith

The new wealth of the people, added to their great faith, resulted in the building of wonderful cathedrals. The dark interiors of some churches were lit by rainbow light from the stained-glass windows.

RUTGER

The Hundred Years' War

It is hard to imagine a war that lasted as long as a hundred years. Few men then lived to that age and only creatures as long-lived as tortoises could see the beginning and end of such a war. But a war did go on for more than a hundred years and it was fought by human beings—their sons, grandsons, and great-grandsons.

At first it was just a war between two kings and their noblemen. The two kings were Edward the Third of England and Philip the Sixth of France. Edward claimed that as his mother was the sister of the last king of France, he himself was the rightful heir to the French throne. As Philip would not give up the throne, Edward declared war on him in 1338. In one year the English looted Poitiers, won Crécy, captured Calais and defeated the Scots in battle.

Yet out of all these victories, they only managed to keep one advantage. Calais became an English town, and stayed that way until the sixteenth century.

Probably the war would not have lasted quite so long had it not been for the Black Death, or bubonic plague. This dreadful disease came from Asia Minor. According to records of the time, it wiped out one quarter of the people in Europe. The plague only halted the war for a time. It did not end it.

Once the plague had died down, the English renewed their assault on France. The king of France was captured and held prisoner in England. But slowly the whole situation changed. Kings died, and were succeeded by new kings. England came to need an ally in Europe, instead of an enemy. The English withdrew from France in the year 1453, after a defeat in battle, and at last there was peace once more in Europe.

Joan of Arc

Behind the great altar of the abbey church at Rheims, in the tomb of a saint, lay a crystal vase, holding a sacred oil. With this holy liquid many of the kings of France had been anointed.

King Henry V was never anointed. When he died, his heir was a baby only nine months old. The way was clear for the Armagnacs, enemies of the English, to put their prince on the throne. This prince, the Dauphin Charles, was a timid, sickly youth, afraid of being king.

A simple peasant girl called Joan of Arc believed she heard heavenly voices speaking to her as she tended her father's sheep. These voices told her she must ride to the city of Orleans, free it from the English, and take the Dauphin to Rheims. Impossible though it seems, Joan succeeded in doing all these things. Knowing nothing of war, she placed herself at the head of the army and led it to victory. Only nine days after her arrival at its walls, Orleans was a free city. The Dauphin was crowned in Rheims Cathedral, and anointed with the sacred oil.

After all this, poor Joan was handed over to the English soldiers. With the help of a French bishop and other churchmen, she was burned to death as a witch. King Charles did not raise a finger to help her.

These pictures, all illustrations from books, are among the very first we have that show scenes from ordinary life in medieval times. People are seen fighting, studying, working in the fields with a plough, and hunting.

Until pictures like these began to appear in books, the only pictures people had to look at were religious paintings and stained glass windows in churches.

Craftsmen and apprentices

We have already talked about the beginning of the guilds. All the members of one guild carried on the same trade. Often they all lived in the same part of a town. In some towns, it is still possible to tell who lived where. There are streets with names like Fishmongers' Row, Shoe Lane, Goldsmiths' Row and Leather Lane.

Members of a guild always promised to uphold the honour of their own guild by the good quality of the things they made or sold. The head of a guild watched over the life and training of the members. He saw that boys worked the right apprenticeship, or period of learning. He laid down the amount of money to be paid to a member when he fell sick, and prices to be charged for goods.

One of the most important things about the guild was the training of young craftsmen. In order to learn his trade, a boy had to live with his master, work with him for years, and obey him in every way. When a young man finished his apprenticeship, he could become a journeyman, moving around and working for craftsmen in the same guild. Only after he had proved his skill by producing very good work could he become a master himself. If a young man was a baker, even a beautifully made loaf of bread could be his masterpiece.

Devils, demons and witches

Although people lived a more civilized life in towns, they still believed in magic. Even the priests of the Church believed in evil spirits, and the dark powers of the Devil. This was not surprising when you remember that there were no scientists who could explain all the strange things that happened in everyday life. The alchemists, still searching for the Elixir of Life, were little help.

Was lightning the wrath of God? Or was it the work of the Devil? Some saw fire as God's gift to man, others saw demons in the flames. And why should a cow or goat suddenly fall ill and die, if it were not the work of a witch? Many poor old women, who talked to themselves, were thought to be witches, muttering evil spells. Such old women often kept a cat. People came to believe these cats were evil spirits, sent by the Devil to help witches in their work. Women who were thought to be witches often had to stand trial by ordeal, and died as a result. At other times they were put in the stocks (pieces of wood with holes for arms and legs). While they were imprisoned in these, people threw stones at them. All Hallow's Eve was supposed to be an important festival for witches. Now it is a time for games, and we call it Hallowe'en.

Golden eggs and magic wands

People believed in evil spirits and in the dark powers of the Devil. They also believed magic could work good. This belief in wonderful magical powers was just as important in peoples' lives as a belief in bad magic.

Even today, when children are young they read and are told fairy tales like "The Goose That Laid the Golden Egg". They know stories and legends about wizards and magicians who can work wonders by the simple touch of a magic wand.

The stories probably began about the same time as ordinary men and women first heard of the work of the

alchemists. These were really the first chemists. They were men who experimented with different kinds of materials. People were no doubt astonished by the work of alchemists. Since they knew nothing about chemistry, they had no reason not to believe that alchemists might really find a way to turn solid rock into gold. There were no scientists around to explain why evil things happened—like cows dying or great storms tearing up trees by the roots. There were also no scientists who could explain strokes of good fortune, or unusual happenings in nature. An ugly cygnet growing up into a beautiful swan must have appeared to be magic. (You know the fairy tale of "The Ugly Duckling".)

If a man found rocks which contained precious stones or streaks of gold, that must have seemed like magic at work.

Slowly, through the centuries, more knowledge of science made the belief in magic less strong. Slowly, men gained a real understanding of the workings of nature. Then man exchanged a belief in science. This happened very close to our own times—in the latter part of the nineteenth century.

The first universities

As the towns grew into cities, people began to take an interest in education. Schools for boys were started in the churches and cathedrals. The teaching in these schools was much the same as that in the earlier monastery schools. It was not what the merchants and craftsmen wanted. In their business, they needed people who could not only read and write, but who could also add and subtract and help them keep their accounts. They began to start schools of their own, to teach boys reading, writing, and arithmetic. These schools, which were open to the sons of tradesmen, were the first "public" schools.

In the larger cities, a new kind of school was started. These were not really schools at all. They were for people who already had an education, but who wanted to learn even more, or to do new research on their special subject. These were the first universities. Unlike present-day universities, they had no large or beautiful buildings, no lecture halls, and no science laboratories full of expensive equipment. Any learned man who thought he had some knowledge worth passing on to others could settle near a school, and give lectures to anyone who would listen to him. Those lecturers who could collect the most students received the most money in fees. Fees collected from students were the lecturers' only income. So the most interesting lecturers were also the richest. As the universities grew, men who wanted to teach had to have a licence. Buildings were also built specially for lectures.

The taste for learning went on growing. Cities that wanted to have a good university tempted lecturers and students by offering them freedom from taxes, and from the laws of the cities. Students and teachers had their own laws, their own courts, and their own prisons. They even spoke their own language, Latin. It was the language in which all the books were written.

Students went to the universities to learn to become doctors, lawyers, or politicians. The first faculty (college) of law was in Bologna, Italy. In England, the universities of Oxford and Cambridge were founded in the Middle Ages.

The age of exploration

Constantinople had fallen into the hands of the Turks. The old trade routes, leading overland from the Mediterranean Sea to Asia, India, and China, were closed to western countries. New routes had to be found.

The Spanish and the Portuguese were the first to send ships from their Atlantic ports to look for a new way round the coast of Africa to India. The Dutch and the English soon followed them. Gone were the days when people hid fearfully behind the thick walls of monasteries and castles. A new age of adventure and exploration was opening up.

Index